David Fenton is a family man married to Anne with twin sons Matthew and James and two younger brothers Tim and Andrew. He loves to combine a 'cause with a challenge' as evidenced by this book. An experienced Marketing Leader with a proven record in delivering marketing transformation in different industries. David enjoys running, is a keen sports fan, and is a passionate Manchester United supporter. David has a B.A. Hons. in Economics & Politics from Durham University and has recently set up his own business.

In loving memory of George Michael "Chips" Fenton 1937–2023.

David Fenton

MILES, MILESTONES AND MEMORIES

AUSTIN MACAULEY PUBLISHERS®

LONDON * CAMBRIDGE * NEW YORK * SHARJAH

A CIP catalogue record for this title is available from the British Library.

ISBN 9781398471320 (Paperback)
ISBN 9781398471337 (ePub e-book)

www.austinmacauley.com

First Published 2025
Austin Macauley Publishers Ltd®
1 Canada Square
Canary Wharf
London
E14 5AA

Thanks to Billie Sharp of innov8 Graphic Design for the front cover.

Taking advantage of a double opportunity created by recent and momentous events; the coronavirus pandemic and losing my job, echoed two other life-changing events stretching back some 23 years ago. This echo was a signal for me to repay a debt. This is the story of my emotional and physical journey of repayment and took the form of tackling a blister-busting hike over 600 miles through fields, roads, suburbs, cities and distinct landmarks of England, for charity—whilst navigating the rapidly escalating coronavirus pandemic and lockdown challenges—and a few unplanned surprises on the way.

Preface

Despite navigating our way in and out of COVID lockdowns throughout 2020, the month of August began like any other typical August month in any year would for me. We returned from a great family holiday week at an apartment that we rented near Charlestown in Cornwall. It was a fantastic week of exploring the local area, enjoying a few drinks and meals out with the family, and generally winding down from the stresses of lockdown musical chairs.

The restrictions caused by the virus were evident but did not negatively impact us too much. We had phoned ahead and booked restaurants given you could not spontaneously turn up for a table. The accommodation was clean, spacious, and all toiletries had to be brought with us rather than using those provided by the apartment. It was fantastic to get away to a new location, enjoy some sunshine, be able to walk along the beaches and explore the local area.

I returned to work from holiday with vigour to wade through the thousands of emails that demanded attention and prepared for the quarterly marketing board meeting, which I chaired. Then normality disappeared…

In the middle of the biggest social and economic crisis in living history—coronavirus—occurred a big personal setback for me with the news that my job was being made redundant. I knew this situation was not unique to me, as many others experienced similar knockbacks with many companies struggling to survive.

What is more personal to me, was the realisation that I could transform the very real, very worrying, situation into an opportunity. The opportunity to walk over 600 miles across England to raise money for charity. Why? This is my story. It covers my journey, physically and emotionally, my reflections, and provides daily bulletins on the evolving context with headline news and COVID updates at the time, the impact this has on my walk, my mood, my thoughts, as well as the race to finish ahead of the lockdown restrictions that worsened day by day.

Introduction

On Thursday, 13 August 2020, there is a hastily arranged video conference for the following day where I am informed that my job has been restructured and my role is being made redundant. Amid the coronavirus pandemic, the timing for me to conjure up a new commercial leadership role of similar stature when all sectors are battening down the hatches, at a time when millions of people are on furlough is not great. I feel disappointed that this has happened and frustrated to be leaving before I have achieved my work goals.

I ask myself could I have done something to cause this or alternatively to mitigate this, but in the battle of emotion versus logic, I try to rationalise that this is a decision made by others, and outside my control. It still hurts though. I am by nature, an optimist and positive, and I want to turn this immediately into an opportunity. I need to use this time that I have been given to give something back whilst pushing myself to use this time and create some kind of legacy.

I am extremely fortunate that I do not need to rush into a job immediately, unlike many others who are facing similar challenges, and so I have this hunger to go and do something different. I want to do something that is physically and mentally challenging for me and that benefits other people. I draw inspiration deeply from iconic historical sources as well as creating my own epiphany:

"A pessimist sees the difficulty in every opportunity; an optimist sees the opportunity in every difficulty" (Winston Churchill) and "Keep moving forwards like the wheels on the bus" (they also go round and round but that is less relevant) (Me).

Mum and Dad: This section shows how hard it was to be made redundant. Although we knew this must be so, David was so upbeat when he spoke to us, you would never have known - he does try and shield us.

December 1997

For the inspiration behind my challenge, I need to go back twenty-three years when my wife, Anne, and I were blessed with twin boys. It is hard now to remember all the details of that time—it felt as if we were walking through treacle and reacting to the events of the moment. It was an exciting time but also one of angst, uncertainty, and a major element of fear of the unknown. Anne was booked into the Royal Berkshire Hospital in Reading for a caesarean as one of the babies (Matthew) was larger than his smaller twin brother (James) and effectively taking all the nutrition for himself—Matthew was growing OK; James had effectively stopped growing.

In future years, of course, we educated Matthew that was not the 'way of things' to take all the good things for himself. The boys were born several weeks prematurely; Matthew was born at 6 pounds and 9 ounces that is not bad, James was only 4 pounds and 2 ounces. Impressive that I can recall these statistics unaided. Both boys had difficulties—Anne and I held them both briefly before James was put into an incubator wired up to various machines and monitors. Matthew was allowed initially to rest in a cot in the recovery room with Anne but was then identified as having some breathing difficulties, so he was also taken into special care. The emotions were all over the place—delight naturally that we had two babies, worry because it was all so new, concern because they were both in special care and fear that we might just get things wrong.

Of course, any parent has a plethora of feelings to deal with—pride that the baby is here, relief that the birth has gone as planned, a feeling that you would do anything or give anything to protect them (which never goes away). There is something else though when they are premature and go into special care. It is an angst, a fear maybe, a sense of helplessness—you are in the hands of others— experts for sure and rightly so—but there is not much you can do. You feel helpless and that is a horrible feeling—it almost feels as if it does not matter what you do or how you do it.

When things are in your control or influence then you can materially affect the outcome. Having premature babies all you can do is wait, listen, and hope things will turn out OK. Everything is doubled of course. Anne was in a neighbouring ward to the boys while I visited every day and tried to juggle work and support for Anne. It was a turbulent rollercoaster of ups and downs and both Matthew and James were in special care—Buscot ward for several days.

We were hoping to be back from the hospital for Christmas, but the boys were not ready—although I think they were out of special care at that point. We had Christmas Day in the hospital, we postponed opening presents until we returned home, and had a Christmas dinner on a tray. Not what we had planned but we were just grateful that both boys were progressing and improving. Looking back now it is hard to recall our feelings. It felt at the time like a whirlwind as if we were the leaves riding the turbulence not quite sure where we were headed and not able to control the direction we took.

In hindsight, I felt a bit like a pound coin. Heads for happiness—two small babies who both had good sets of lungs on them, and we were a family with a future ahead of us that was up for shaping. Tails for the fear—could we really do it? Could we nurture and nourish them, help them know what is right and wrong, good, and bad? Even today Anne muddles her left from her right—when navigating in the car she sometimes indicates the direction I should take with her hand—and Anne is the teacher and the more sensible of the two of us.

We left the Royal Berkshire Hospital for home on 27 December 1997. What kept us going over that period was two things—the support of our close friends and family who all came to visit and the support of the nurses in the Buscot ward. Even today I can recall the warmth of the staff, their empathy, the sensitive way they impart information, their understanding, their reassurance whilst not making any false promises. I recall the corridors covered in thank you letters and colourful pictures.

Anne and I were so appreciative of this support and committed to each other that at some point in the future we wanted to give 'something back' to help other parents in a similar situation. Now when I look at the boys today and what they have achieved I could not be prouder. The memories and the feelings and emotions they evoke came back vividly to me resurfacing a few years ago as my younger brother Andrew and his wife Hilary had their children who also spent their early days in special care and are now thriving toddlers. Anne and I vowed to raise funds to help support other new parents who find themselves in this situation.

The other driving force to give something back is to support my younger brother Tim who has had some health challenges with Sarcoidosis that can affect the heart and lungs.

Sarcoidosis is a rare condition that causes small patches of red and swollen tissue, called granulomas, to develop in the organs of the body. It usually affects the lungs and skin. (source NHS)

For many people with sarcoidosis, symptoms often improve without treatment within a few months or years. For these people, the symptoms are not usually severe.

However, a few people find their symptoms develop gradually and get worse over time, to the point where they become severely affected. This is known as chronic sarcoidosis, and this is what Tim has. There is currently no cure, but symptoms can usually be managed with medicine. When I asked him which charity he would like to support; the British Heart Foundation was his clear unequivocal response.

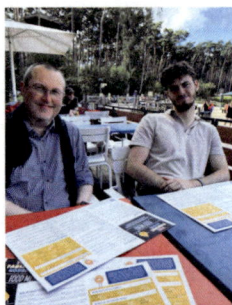

Tim: "I don't dwell too much on what I've been through health wise but suffice to say I got a rare disease that impacted the function of my heart. I received 1st class medical care from the NHS and am fortunately much recovered. I benefited hugely from past medical heart research that enabled many of the treatments I received. The British Heart Foundation continue to fund this research today and seemed a natural fit for David to contribute to, so that others benefit as I have done."

So Where Will the Money Raised Go To?

50% will go to BIBS and 50% to the British Heart Foundation.

"**Babies in Buscot Support (BIBS)** raise funds to give sick and premature new-born babies at the Royal Berkshire Hospital the best possible start in life. The donations will be used to support all our work, which focuses on four main areas of activity that together we call keeping Buscot families 'SAFE' (Support, Awareness, Facilities and Equipment) The charity is run entirely by parents that have had a baby spend time on Buscot Ward. Thank you for helping #SaveTinyLives." More info: *www.bibs.org.uk*

The **British Heart Foundation** "our vision is a world free from the fear of heart and circulatory diseases. We raise money to research cures and treatments, so we can beat heartbreak forever. We fund over £100 million of research each year into all heart and circulatory diseases and the things that cause them." More info: *bhf.org.uk*

I have set myself an initial target to raise £2,000. All food and accommodation costs will be self-funded, or if possible sponsored, so I can donate all the contributions to the two charities.

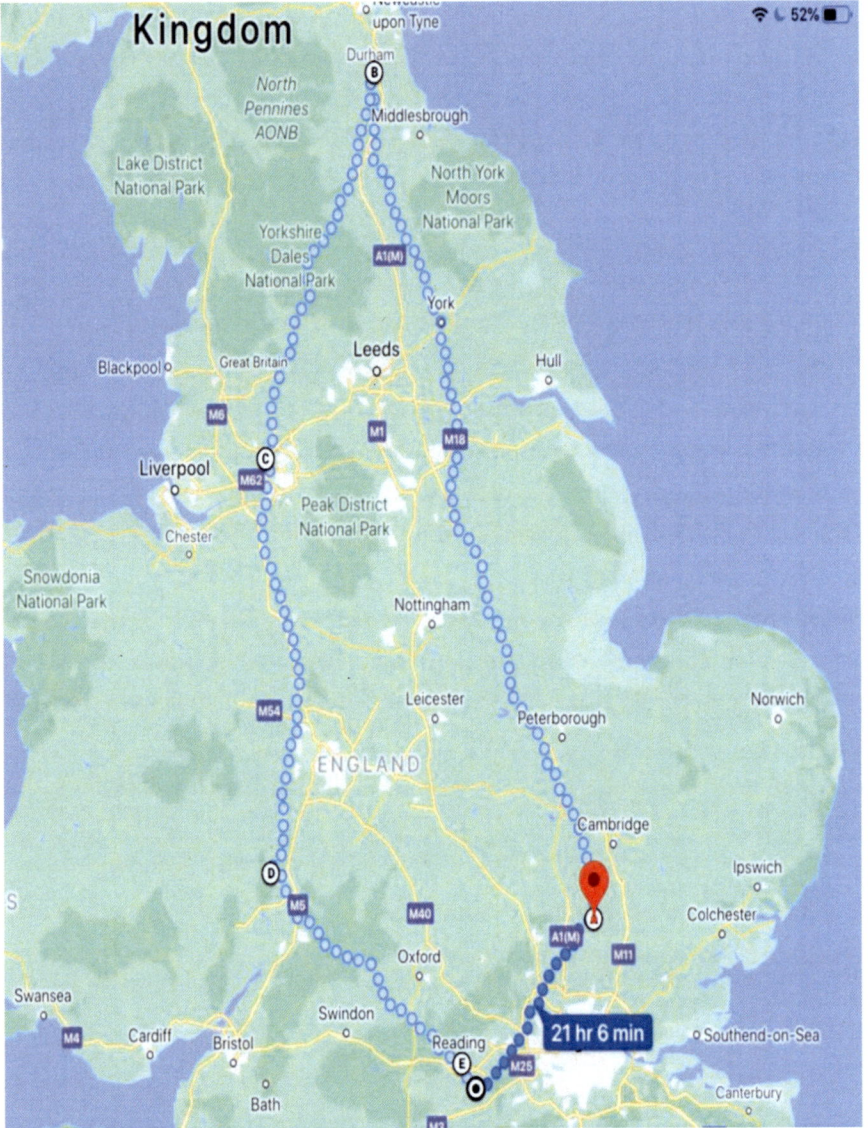

600+ mile route via places of interest.

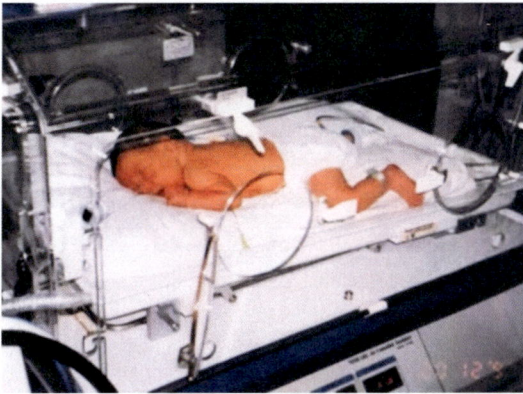

Matthew (December 1997).

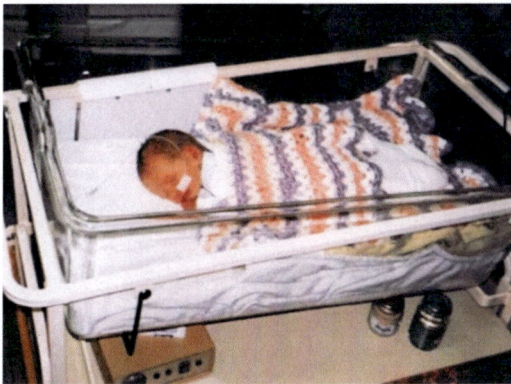

James (December 1997).

Cheeky twins aged 2.

Cheeky twins aged 20.

Proud moments receiving Gold Duke of Edinburgh certificates.

The Challenge

Which brings me back to today—and leveraging both my desire and time to raise funds for both the charities. I considered a cycling challenge. I have always enjoyed cycling and indeed have been part of the notorious (in the world of builders' merchants) Tour De Jewson that involves employees, customers and suppliers cycling between Jewson branches from one end of the country to the other in order to raise funds for charity. However, the thought of cycling with a large rucksack on my back puts me off.

I decide on a walking challenge to raise the funds. I want it to be a 'big' challenge that tests me mentally and physically so that I feel a sense of pain, a sense of not being in full control, a sense of achievement as I overcome the barriers—as well as to raise the funds that is the ultimate goal. I contemplate walking the perimeter of the UK or walking to the capitals of England, Scotland, and Wales. I have some history of walking having completed the Yorkshire 3 peaks and been part of the Jewson management team who completed a couple of week-long treks to raise funds for charity a few years ago.

Anne comes up with the great idea that is what we go with—ironically while we are out for a local walk for exercise—which is to visit places that are important to me over the course of my life. I like that idea. After 24 years of marriage, I have tried to perfect the art of 'active listening', however, I confess to the occasional 'nod and grunt' approach when Anne is in a verbose mood and sometimes, I get caught out when she poses a question at the end of her point.

My agreement with her idea of the 'walk theme' shows that sometimes I do listen. I begin to work out the route using Google Maps, and I will be doing over 600 miles in 30 days based on walking 6 out of 7 days per week. This translates into five milestones—more of which are to come later.

Over 600 miles! Now that sounds like a physical and mental challenge. Well, I do not think the Proclaimers were ambitious enough in walking only 500 miles.

19 Days Before the Walk

Practice Walk 1—Wednesday 26 August 2020.

I get a lot of 'advice' from Anne so am fortunate enough to get a lot of pointers on what I need to think about ahead of the walk. I agree that some practice walks are a good idea. Knowing that my target mileage is 25–30 miles a day, I think an 18-mile trial run—or should that be 'trial walk'—would be good preparation. I will be undertaking the walk in the middle of the pandemic.

The restrictions caused by COVID do not overly concern me and will be annoying rather than prohibitive. I will need to be careful and follow the social distancing rules, but I will be pre-booking accommodation ahead of my scheduled miles and we are no longer in lockdown—plus in September the weather should generally be warm. I am excited.

Anne and I arrange to meet some friends Nigel and Julie in Marlow for lunch—so I have a nice incentive at the end of it. My first practice walk, and it is a beautiful sunny day, I walk in my running trainers and do not get any blisters so, all in all, it is a particularly good start. This is a great way for me to test what works once I get going on the full walk. I use Google Maps that gives me different route options on the roads and bridleways although it does not pick up footpaths.

I feel excited and a little anxious as I set off, as it means I have progressed from theory into practice. It is getting close to reality now as my journey starts in less than two weeks but at the same time, I am committed to it. I do not want to say I will do something and then not do it. I pass through some lovely villages in the sunshine—I particularly enjoy the rural off-road section that is so peaceful and picturesque.

I find it very strange to come across an airfield in the middle of nowhere—well that may be unfair to White Waltham—but an array of small planes is lined up ready to take off. My experience of airfields is more queues of traffic approaching Heathrow (usually business) or Gatwick (usually holidays). Today is quite windy and as I adjust my phone to take the photographs my cap blows off my head and bounces across the viewing area.

With winds like this, I am glad to be travelling on my own two feet and not up in the strong air currents. I do not profess to be an ace photographer but as I approach the Maidenhead area, I observe perspectives I would never ordinarily notice—the natural colour differences between the grey and white cloudy sky contrasting the green and brown of the fields and trees–a rich tapestry of colour. I also enjoy the transition from rural areas to villages or towns. Today walking past the Compleat Angler on the outskirts of Marlow brings back memories of my niece's christening a couple of years ago.

My brother Andrew and his wife Hilary christened their first child, Aoife, in Marlow with the reception at the Compleat Angler bringing both families, from England and Ireland, together for a great day. Oh, the joys of travel and getting together with loved ones! I do not see many boats on the Thames–like the sunshine they seem to have disappeared. I am first to arrive in Marlow, so I can have a caffeine boost from a local coffee shop while I sit and wait for Anne, Julie, and Nigel to arrive.

One of the advantages of walking is that I do not have to try and find a parking space. I feel upbeat, my legs are OK, and I could have walked further– now I can enjoy a well-deserved lunch and catch up with our friends. The impact of COVID in the restaurant is clear with sanitiser at the door, all the staff wearing masks and following the two-metre social distancing rules and a one-way route to and from the loos—but there is an upside as we take advantage of the 'eat out to help out' scheme.

Editor note: For each entry in the journal I have included a summary of the News headlines along with a Covid update to illustrate the context of my challenge.

News Headlines Context, 26 August 2020 (Source for All Daily Headlines: Reach News Archive)

The head of the English exams board Sally Collier steps down as a result of the handling of A levels and GCSEs. Meanwhile, Boris Johnson accuses the BBC of 'wetness' over Last Night of the Proms. The Prime Minister expresses disbelief at the broadcaster's decision to perform Rule Britannia and Land of Hope and Glory without lyrics.

COVID Daily Context, 26 August 2020 (Source for All Daily COVID Headlines: Reach News Archive)

"Professor Hugh Pennington compared the coronavirus crisis with the Spanish flu outbreak. Professor Pennington stated that he did not expect to see a second wave of COVID-19 but that the first wave will continue to result in outbreaks. In 1918, when the Spanish flu struck, the first wave was relatively minor, it happened in the summer, the virus went away and then in the late autumn and winter it came back and killed millions of people."

Tracking new cases 1,352; deaths 11

(source: coronavirus.data.gov.uk)

Let us hope there is no second wave with this virus!

My practice walk does not make the front-page news headlines, but on 26 August, there is a ray of hope for a COVID vaccine with Cambridge University receiving £1.9 m from the Government and potentially starting trials in the Autumn.

White Waltham airfield.

The Compleat Angler Marlow.

Arriving in Marlow.

13 Days Before the Walk

Practice Walk 2—Tuesday 1 September 2020

Today is my first day officially unemployed. It feels very strange to be packing a rucksack with cereal bars and water rather than a laptop. James and Anne suggest I should try the full daily mileage with a fully loaded rucksack—i.e., plan for a 'typical walking day'. A very sensible idea and another example of my rapidly improving 'listening skills'.

I identify a route targeting 30 miles to the village of Upton Grey—there and back. Again, I am fortunate that it is another lovely sunny day. I enjoy walking on the bridleway path off Nine Mile Ride in Finchampstead where the sunshine coming through the trees gives a magical, colourful halo. I particularly enjoy the silhouette of the horse captured through a gap in the foliage (see below) with the sun shining in the background. It is a view I would never see when driving a car and the photograph looks almost professional to me.

I have a problem today, however, as I use my 'old favourite' walking boots and develop a couple of big blisters on both feet in Bramshill within 5 miles of setting off. I switch to my running shoes and put on a couple of Compeed (the start of a close relationship between Compeed and myself) and my feet are more comfortable in the softer canvas. Bramshill is a lovely location as it is a large expanse of trees and open areas—I enjoy cycling through here with Matthew and James at weekends, although today it is just me, my rucksack, and my blisters. I arrive at Upton Grey but cannot find a pub or a village centre so turnaround and get a late lunch at a pub in Hook.

I finish the walk but must admit my feet are not in great shape at the end of the day, however, the upside is that I know that I can do it. I find myself reflecting on the walk to come. I am excited about the journey and the discoveries ahead. I know I am fit and can do the mileage as per my practice walks—I am a little less sure that I can do it day in, day out and what the wear and tear will be on my feet as there is not much recovery time. It is exciting also to be visiting places that I have not visited for many years and yet also to be visiting towns and villages that I have never been to before!

News Headlines Context, 1 September 2020

Headlines focus on the new BBC boss with calls for him to help save the free TV licence fees for the elderly (I don't fall into that bracket quite yet) *and Michel Barnier is back to renew discussions on the Brexit trade deal.*

COVID Daily Context, 1 September 2020

Boris Johnson's coronavirus plan to get people back into offices has been met with anger as Professor Chris Whitty threatens to quit. Despite fears of more outbreaks of the deadly virus, Mr Johnson claimed 'huge numbers' of people are now returning to offices and 'quite right too'.

"While a cough has been listed as one of the main symptoms of the virus, a new study has suggested a more likely sign in children. Coronavirus symptoms are listed by the NHS as a high temperature, a new, continuous cough, and a loss or change to your sense of smell or taste. But a new study has found another possible sign in children—an upset tummy."

Tracking new cases 2,249; deaths 3
(source coronavirus.data.gov.uk)

Well, I am definitely enjoying being out of the office currently. With regard to the COVID backdrop, it appears Portugal is about to be added to the quarantine list but fortunately that is not on my scheduled walk this time. It seems there is a conflict between the scientific advice that highlights the virus risk and the economic pressures to enable commerce. The number of new cases is accelerating and while the number of deaths is low, each one is such an acutely painful loss for the families involved.

Bridleway in Finchampstead.

Horse silhouette.

Bramshill forest—great for hide and seek.

9 Days Before the Walk

Practice Walk 3—Friday 4 September 2020

A good friend of mine, Will, is planning a charity walk abroad and has used the services of TrekHire UK so I immediately contact them and arrange to join one of their practice walks in the Surrey hills. Will and his wife Frances have been good friends of ours since we met 23 years ago during NCT classes as their eldest son is the same age as Matthew and James. Mick and Elaina who own the business are fantastic people, and I highly recommend them, they are very friendly, fun, and so helpful. I love the sign outside their shop as it seems particularly appropriate—'Nothing ventured nothing gained'.

I join Will, Mick, and his walkers on a 10-mile walk during which time we have a long chat, and he points me in the right direction with regard to the kit, water bladder, clothing, emergency communications and most importantly footwear. Mick seems to know every footpath available to walk in the Surrey Hills although he tells me that even last week, he came across a new one; that must be fun to have a 'Christopher Columbus' type explorer moment. Mick and Elaina spend a further couple of hours with me after the walk—they sell me walking boots, shoes and socks and lend me a day rucksack and trendy hat (well when I say trendy, I mean relative to some of my other headgear).

For the day's walk itself, I use my running shoes again and no further damage occurs to my feet. I am worried about my feet more than any other aspect. I hope the new footwear will minimise any issues, but I had not expected my old boots to give me the blisters that they did and on previous long fund-raising walks such as the Jewson Jaunts I have had blisters. I have historically done 'bursts' of walking activity—this time with over 600 miles, it is more of an 'explosion' of walking, and I will not fully know if my feet will survive until it is happening.

News Headlines Context, 4 September 2020

Headlines cover the BBC spending millions in order to recoup licence fees; Michel Barnier does not appear to be interested in the UK fishing plans as part of the potential Brexit solution.

COVID Daily Context, 4 September 2020

With regard to the COVID backdrop the estimates are that there were 400 deaths a day in care homes at the height of the virus, and if mass testing works then Christmas hugs are on the agenda! People with coronavirus symptoms have been unable to get home-testing kits in the south-east and instead been told to travel miles to testing centres. Some people, who have been showing symptoms, have been told there are no tests available for several days in a row. The Government is closely monitoring coronavirus cases across the country and has been implementing local lockdowns for areas with increases in cases. In what has been dubbed the 'whack a mole' strategy, towns, cities and regions can be placed under lockdown to prevent further spread. Leicester, Trafford, Bolton, parts of West Yorkshire and East Lancashire are currently under stricter rules than the rest of the country due to a rise in cases.

"Now, areas across the North of England, more specifically the North East are being watched closely after an increase in cases week on week. Coronavirus has reportedly mutated. The viral spike protein on SARS-CoV-2 has been observed and named—D6146—which could have influenced its ability to spread more easily."

Tracking new cases 3,040; deaths 7
(source coronavirus.data.gov.uk)

I am not sure who comes up with names such as D6146 for a virus—they hardly trip off the tongue—maybe they get lost in translation as words get muffled via the facemask ending up sounding more like a character from a Dr Who episode. I am starting to worry a bit more about the virus and its potential implications. The north-east is mentioned as being under review and this is one of the zones I am planning to visit. The local lockdown approach could potentially cause me issues depending on the extent of the restrictions.

It is challenging to plan contingency options at this point as I do not know which areas will be impacted and which will be OK, which means planning my fallback routes is nigh on impossible. I will carry on with my current plan and in the evenings after my day's walk then I can recalculate my route if necessary. It sounds easy, but in practice, it could mean multiple changes to accommodation depending on which locations are open and if they will put me up. It adds to the tension and element of surprise though.

Love the sign—sums up my adventure.

Me with the group—Abinger Hammer.

Resume   **Save Activity**

Distance	Pace	Time
11.7 km	**15:35 /km**	**3h 3m**

CUSTOMIZE YOUR WALK

Name: Title your walk

     Add photos to your walk

Sport: **Walk**

Commute

Save Activity

Strava route download in Surrey Hills.

Planning

As well as practice walks, I spend a lot of time route planning, although even then probably not enough, (editor note: as you will hear about later). I end up with ten versions of my route plan. I use Google Maps to plot the various legs and miles—25–30 miles per day with several rest days scheduled. Leg 1 is coming out at 63 miles, leg 2 is the scary one of 235 miles, leg 3 will be 111 miles, leg 4, funnily enough, would also be 111 miles with leg 5 easier (apart from the navigation of the Cotswolds!) at 96 miles.

My principal concern is carrying a heavy load on my back and managing my feet. I have a long kit list—I can borrow a lot of clothing from my sons Matthew and James that they have used previously during the Duke of Edinburgh Award Expeditions. It is a kind of ironic role reversal as the children generally dress up in their parent's clothes although it is pleasing that I fit into their kit. I think that I may have way too much gear.

Anne helps me set up the Virgin Money Giving Page that is a great way to manage the money that I raise with no hassle, and she sets up a Facebook page where we can update the daily progress. I contact pubs, guesthouses, B&Bs to ask if they will donate a bed for the night. I use Google Maps to identify the right distance and then get onto the phone.

There are four types of responses that I get. Many places that I call are only too willing to help and generously agree to put me up for a night that is fantastic. The second group are those that are willing but not able, due to being booked up. The third group is those that are unable to help me, and these are generally national chains that have their own charity programmes. The fourth is a category where the B&B's 'do not even exist'.

After a while, I get to spot the type as on Google Maps, they often have a picture of a field, a strange name, and they rarely answer the phone. My order of preference is always pub followed by guesthouse or B&B followed by national hotel chain (as I will have to pay). Overall, I am blown away by the generosity of small businesses that have never met me. It feels close now as it's less than a week until I depart. I feel confident in myself—I have the gear, and I know what I need to do.

It is the small things that form a continual niggle or doubt. What if I lose my phone or it runs out of charge? I have the fallback of a second phone borrowed from James but have not got physical maps, for example, as I am going to so many different places. Without a phone and a signal then I cannot navigate. Another worry is when I get comments from others—the intentions of the advice are good, but it creates seeds of doubt in my mind. Anne passed on a comment around the height and the rate of incline of the Yorkshire Dales and that the number of miles I am planning is fine for the flat but not going upwards.

My other worry is the rucksack transport. The large rucksack is heavy, although manageable, at least it was for one day, and I have not tested repeating that weight day after day; I hope that I can organise either a lift from a helpful landlord or a taxi who will transport it at a small cost to the next location. None of the companies who specialise in shipping or deliveries responded to my pleas for help so I will sort it out at the time. At least in certain locations, then Anne, my parents, friends will be able to help.

On the other hand, despite these niggles, I just want to get on with it and then I can adjust if necessary.

4 Days Before the Walk

Final Practice Walk 4—Wednesday 9 September 2020

My final practice walk is with my buddy Will on Wednesday 9 September. We have a lovely day as the weather is bright and sunny and we walk 20 miles in six hours from Sunningdale to Windsor and back via Virginia Water. We make good going and the new walking boots are comfortable, although I still have some blister remnants to manage from the Upton Grey practice walk. We manage to find a lovely pub to recuperate in for a pie and pint (great timing as the '50% eat out to help out' scheme is still on in that pub). We walk back through Windsor Great Park and Virginia Water, so we see some fantastic views; it is great to have Will's company and be able to chat or walk in companionable silence.

I also successfully get to grips with the Strava settings without requiring technical help from Matthew or James (Will is a similar level to me so not much help in that matter). Strava is an internet service for tracking human exercise that incorporates social network features. It is mostly used for cycling and running using GPS data. It has a lot of social connection opportunities—for example, Will and I can track each other's walking routes and statistics, however, my main use is to track the mileage (rather than kilometres) as well as tracking the elevation and average speed to check my progress versus the plan.

News Headlines Context, 9 September 2020

Headlines show angst in Europe and in the UK over Boris Johnson's plan to break international law to deal with Northern Ireland as part of Brexit. On climate, the earth is already close to exceeding the temperatures set out in the Paris Accord.

"At a Downing Street press conference on Wednesday, Mr Johnson unveiled new rules that ban social gatherings of more than six people, insisting they are aimed at averting a second lockdown. The rule applies to meetings both outdoors and indoors, in people's homes as well as public venues. The Prime Minister said 'COVID-secure marshals' would be sent out to patrol streets to ensure the measures are being respected."

Tracking new cases 3,330; deaths 9

(source coronavirus.data.gov.uk)

Ready to go.

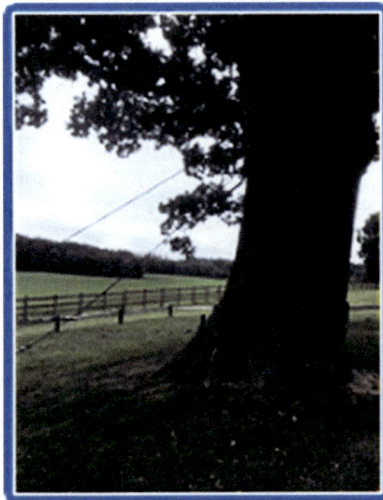

A couple of ropes to keep the tree vertical.

Will and myself—both smiling.

Virginia Water.

This is where walking on my own fits nicely within the rules—still, scope to find 'five friends' as my walk evolves. It is clearly a very fine line to tread between the interests of the health practitioners and scientists whose priority is life and death versus the commercial impact of the economic considerations—cases and deaths are continuing to rise, and I am not at all sure how this will impact my schedule—but I am sure it will.

Both Anne and I reach out to several companies—and celebrities with either a link to walking or premature babies—for potential sponsorship but with limited success. The commercial reality is that many companies have had to cut back on their marketing spend so I understand the timing is not great from that point of view. I write to manufacturers of the gear I am using; the most successful approach is to NAKD bars who supply me with plenty of nutrition with several boxes of bars to top up my 'munchies' and they are delicious too. The banoffee pie bar wins me over quickly. I did not get any responses from the celebrities although it could be that their admin teams did not forward the request for help.

We also leverage our respective networks to target donations and to get additional followers for the Facebook page. We have so many people donate via the page including family, friends, colleagues, strangers. I target my network on LinkedIn and Anne sets up a community on Facebook that we use to post daily updates. It sounds simple but it is not. Many donors are not on Facebook, so we replicate the updates on Viber, Instagram, and WhatsApp.

Two Days Before Arriving at Milestone One

Day 1. Sunday 13 September 2020, Finchampstead to Chalfont St Giles

I am very keen and excited to get up and get off so set the alarm for 6:30, have my final breakfast at home and set off by 7:30. Anne kindly offers to transport my kit in the 85-litre rucksack to my first hotel stop meaning that I can use the smaller day rucksack with only the essentials on my back with no problem. I am blessed with a lovely sunny day and a great start to the walk (using my walking shoes). About 5 miles in however I feel some discomfort on my feet with a couple of blisters forming, and I realise I have made a schoolboy error. I have removed my customised insoles that had been fitted by Mick at TrekHire UK that match the profile of my feet.

I must have left the insoles in my other pair of walking boots, which are in the large rucksack when I was sorting my kit, and which Anne will transport to my hotel later. I have not even inserted the standard insoles back into the walking shoes, so I am walking without any insoles at all. Not a smart move. In fact, a stupid move after all the planning that I have been doing. I place an emergency phone call to the 'support team' (Anne) to bring the large rucksack out to me on the road and which has my walking boots with the customised insoles.

While I am waiting, I apply a pair of my trusty Compeed—which are incredibly good and immediately make a difference—and it is great now to have the comfortable support of the insoles on both feet. This is a very silly mistake as I know my feet are my main tool for the walk, and I am off to a bad start by damaging them on the morning of the first day. I will not repeat this error—I just hope I do not come to regret it.

I have a fantastic surprise when two fellows approach me on the pavement around halfway through the day's walk—I think I recognise them from a distance, and I do. Matthew and James are staying away overnight at a mate's house and using the location service on their phone discover that I am only 2 miles away. So they join me, and we have a snack at the nearby pub. A lovely surprise and a nice break.

It is maybe an omen to see the boys today as ultimately it is because of them that I am doing this walk. It is incredible to look back at the photos from when they are a few days old and lying-in incubators to walking alongside them into the pub–they are nearly as tall as me (but not quite). Both Anne and I are incredibly proud of them.

The journey of raising children is like the walk I am undertaking in many ways. There is a sense of purpose and a sense of direction, but often you have no idea what is immediately around the next corner. There are highs and lows, tears and laughter, achievement of milestones and ultimately progress is made!

As I reflect, I realise that I really enjoy all the different phases of childhood. The early years when they cling to you, and you have their full respect if not adoration. I recall mowing the grass of our back lawn in our first house with the boys and both following in my trail pushing their plastic lawnmowers. While Matthew was calm and more sedate (and did not go on the so-called naughty step at school), James was very active, always mobile and could not sit still (and was occasionally on the 'naughty step'). We were pleased once when eventually Matthew was put on the step although I cannot recall why.

At pre-school, there was a definite low point when I took time off work to accompany Anne and other parents to watch their first 'play'. We were quite excited and full of anticipation until the end of the play arrived, and there had been no sign of either boy. When we went 'backstage' (i.e., behind the curtain) we found them both asleep as they were exhausted and so missed the whole event sleeping on the floor. We were both extremely disappointed, and I went back to work deflated. I am still not sure how the nursery assistants managed to delegate their acting roles so quickly to other toddlers.

I really loved the school years and watching them play a sport from the touchline. They also played for the local football and cricket teams. It was great to watch them mature and to chat with the parents of their friends—even today I miss that.

Again, we experienced several highs—Matthew as the goalkeeper at Finchampstead football club saving several penalties in a shootout for a cup game and winning the 'players' player' of the season. James was the captain of the Finchampstead football team at 12 and later won a silver medal in the

National Schools Regatta held at the National Watersports Centre, Holme Pierrepont. Great memories. But there were also lows—both boys being carted off from various matches in an ambulance for example. Matthew having landed on his neck in a rugby match, a very worrying time—and James for a damaged leg in a football match. The former was particularly concerning (although turned out fine) and the latter was highly inconvenient at the time as they were playing in different matches against the same school, and I needed to split my time between them. I watched Matthew in the first half and then James got his injury just before I could watch his match in the second half. A call from the school on a Wednesday afternoon when a sport was on the agenda was often a worry and usually resulted in Anne collecting one of them to take for an x-ray.

Both Matthew and James are bright and have achieved great results academically. I am particularly proud of them achieving the Gold Duke of Edinburgh's Award, as you must develop and demonstrate a range of skills and complete challenging expeditions; it is not for the faint-hearted. The photo of the four of us in London for the boys to receive their certificates from the Duke of Edinburgh at St James' Palace is one of those 'magic moments'. It is also a real benefit to have twins in this case as each child is limited to taking one parent as their guest—so fortunately with two children, we could both go.

The ceremony that we attended was made even more special as it was the final time that the Duke of Edinburgh gave out the awards before he retired. He was already well into his 90s and appeared very robust and welcoming. Gareth Malone also attended as a special guest. As we waited for the Duke to arrive in the room in which our school group were waiting, he got us all singing a three-part song with the children and their parents. Neither Matthew nor I have a tuneful voice unlike James and Anne, but we can all claim to have sung with Gareth Malone in the presence of royalty—now how is that for a claim to fame?

Matthew and James are so much more rounded than I was at their age. They are both good cooks that blends well with my washing up skills; I can do a mean roast dinner, omelette, and curry (with sauce from a jar), and not all blended together, but that is about it. I have evolved though.

I recall when I went inter-railing across Europe one summer holiday while I was at university. I travelled with a couple of mates and took my turn at the occasional meal when forced to. One time it was my turn to cook spaghetti, which I had not cooked before; I could not work out how to get the long strings of spaghetti into a small pan sitting on top of a small camping gas stove. I was caught cutting up the spaghetti sticks with a pair of scissors so that they would fit in the pan.

Then as they grow older the 'parental idolising' disappears and their negotiation techniques improve. Your role as a parent becomes more of a provider and chauffeur. For me, there are four distinct phases in the evolution of child-parent negotiation:

Phase one—when they are new-borns, and they just cry to get what they want. In fact, it is not even negotiation as there is no give and take or win/win scenario—it is all about 'I want' expressed through tears and screaming. For us, it was often in stereo. There is no choice other than to give in as 'the negotiation' revolves around food, nappies or sleep and you must provide an answer.

The negotiation frequently ended up with me taking one or both out in the car to drive them around until they dropped off (hopefully before I did). I heard about one set of parents who would remove the sleeping child from the car and position the car seat with the sleeping baby still in it, in the middle of the double bed between the two parents.

Phase two—the toddler phase. Often highly amusing but when they are two or three years old, they see the negotiation as equating to willpower. Being stubborn or resilient is clearly a trait useful in negotiations but it requires some variety. Matthew, in particular, favoured this approach.

I recall one holiday in Wales where we hired a cottage with my parents and brothers and respective families. It was a lovely cottage and had a squash court that we utilised for getting the kids to run around when it was raining outside. One event stands out very clearly when Matthew was frustrated as he wanted to keep the ball to himself, and he could not get hold of it, as it bounced around the walls of the court with five or six of us passing it between the group. So proceeded thirty minutes of very loud wailing or should I say 'howling' from Matthew.

The howling echoed around the walls of the court and could be heard by Grandma who was in the adjoining cottage. Of course, he could not get his way as that would reward the intransigent 'negotiation technique'.

Phase three—the teenage phase. Another highly amusing phase occurs as teenagers push and probe and try new techniques. This phase is often accompanied by the 'If I do this, will you do that' phase. They understand the two-way approach to negotiation and that in order to get what they want; something must be given back. The subtlety tends to improve over time. Both

Matthew and James excelled in this phase such that you are no longer conscious of the power transfer from parents to children.

The consequence of course is lifts to parties, extending the bedtimes, the occasional taste of alcohol, letting them play computer games that are one or two years older than they are (but not 18s!). Of course, one amusing aspect is to utilise them in your own negotiations. Sometimes this worked and sometimes not. So, if I wanted to watch an action film such as *Star Wars* (whereas Anne would not) then the boys could be incredibly useful in pushing that agenda as their idea.

Phase four—adulthood. In many ways, this is like phase one but without the howling. They are now masters of negotiation. They know your strengths and weaknesses and are able to manipulate without the grownups being aware. They turn the tables and may use me as the Trojan horse to take on negotiations on their behalf if it involves sport or a barbeque. Similarly, if it involves clothes, friends, presents then they will use Anne to accomplish their goals. Often this phase is 'win' rather than 'win-win'.

It is interesting how the parental role of the coach begins to reverse in key areas where the child becomes the coach. One of the last areas where I could pass on my knowledge, and they would listen to me, was when I took them for driving practice at the age of seventeen. Again, I really enjoyed that quality time with them, and I am reasonably patient. James was slightly more confident and faster, whereas Matthew was more considered and cautious.

Yet in the same car and doing similar speeds the magnetic L plates flew off the car several times with Matthew and never with James. It would mean me running back half a mile down the road to pick up the plate and then jog back to him. On one occasion, I could not find the missing plate, so we drove home with only one plate on the car, and I had to purchase another set because you cannot buy just one L plate.

I have subsequently had many amusing moments whenever I come across an L plate on the roadside; I always take a photograph and send it to Matthew, claiming that I have found the missing plate. The fact that this could be anywhere in the country amuses me even further. I say amusing because it usually makes me laugh out loud.

The expertise is clearly reversed in other areas—they became the coach to me in technology, social media, and IT to name but a few. Playing games on PlayStation is another. There was a time that we were reasonably well matched to play a football tournament. I even won one or two. Now, every tournament I get knocked out in the early rounds even when I get the first choice of teams, but after a few weeks, I forget how painful it is and come back for more.

In my mind, I hope that I have improved and can still show them a trick or two. Usually, I concentrate on defence and hope for a 0-0 draw followed by penalties. I was informed recently that if a player loses by a five-goal margin then a letter must be written by the defeated individual to the victor. I am not sure if this is a true rule or just something they have made up for me.

Anyway, in our last tournament, I lost a game by 6-0 and ended up having to write a letter to James to apologise for my poor performance—totally humiliating. Perhaps it's a sign of the times (oh my, I am sounding like my Grandma) but Matthew did ask me recently where on the envelope does the stamp go so I can still add value. I guess there are still many corners to turn and hills to climb or descend….

The rest of the walk is very pleasant although annoyingly the Strava app, which I use on the older phone today does not save properly so I will use the other phone tomorrow. I arrive at the White Hart in Chalfont St Giles to a lovely room kindly donated along with breakfast. In addition, the manager generously donates the bill for my dinner and a couple of pints—a fantastic gesture and much appreciated.

I can sit in the beer garden wearing my flip-flops to help my feet 'air' and reflect on the day including the strange sight of a bicycle stuck halfway up a telegraph pole (must be owned by a circus clown or gymnast). Another family sitting nearby overhear my challenge and kindly donate to my collection tin (and it is a note rather than coins so much easier to carry)—this is my first actual physical donation, and it feels great.

Andrew: I called David 3 times on his first day of walking with each call starting off with an increasingly familiar pattern of "how are you doing?" followed reasonably swiftly with a "so where are you now?". Having lived many years in Berkshire, I was trying to picture exactly where David was by his description. It was increasingly obvious that either his description of geography, or my own geography knowledge did not match. I'll stop asking him where he is when I call tomorrow, I thought. I could tell from the excitement in his voice that he had not only arrived but was basking in the company of a beer. I felt like joining him immediately and this would not be the only time I felt this.

News Headlines Context, 13 September 2020

In news headlines Guy Verhofstadt, Chair of the Brexit steering group has pleaded with the EU to urgently hold a conference to discuss the future of the Brussels bloc as he warns 'European values are beleaguered on all sides'. ANTARCTICA scientists discovered a number of bizarre creatures below the ice 'like nothing they'd seen before' during a fascinating journey through the surrounding waters of the icy continent.

COVID Daily Context, 13 September 2020

Coronavirus infections are on the rise in more than 200 local authorities in England, according to the latest figures, sparking fears of a second wave. Coronavirus figures released by Public Health England reveal 210 of the 315 local authority areas in England (66%) have recorded an increase in weekly cases. Birmingham, Bolton and Blackburn with Darwen, have all reported a surge in new transmissions in the past seven days to 10 September. In Birmingham, there have been more than 1,000 new cases of COVID-19.

A total of 1,014 new cases were recorded—the equivalent of 88.8 cases per 100,000 people, up from 53.0 in the previous week. The alarming figure is significantly above 20 thresholds, which has been enough for most countries to be struck off the UK's safe travel list. Tough new measures banning people from mixing with other households inside and in gardens will be imposed in the city from Tuesday.

"West Midlands mayor Andy Street announced the ban on households mixing in Birmingham, Sandwell and Solihull, following talks with Health Secretary Matt Hancock on Friday. On Monday, the whole of England will be subjected to tighter restrictions with a number 'rule of six' enforced. Prime Minister Boris Johnson announced as of 14 September, it will be illegal to meet in groups of more than six people both indoors and outdoors."

Tracking new cases 2,143; deaths 16

(source: coronavirus.data.gov.uk)

Fortunately, Birmingham is not on my schedule for this walk, but the direction of travel for the virus seems to be only one way, and I am not sure yet how this will affect me as I go progress northwards. The rate of infections has nearly doubled since I started my practice walks, and the rate of death is now five times higher.

Braywick Pub in Taplow.

With Matthew and James.

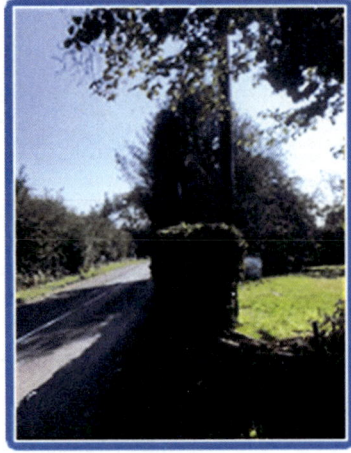

Impressive bike manoeuvring on a telegraph pole.

One Day Before Arriving at Milestone One

Day 2. Monday 14 September 2020, Chalfont St Giles to Welwyn

I start the day off with a delicious, cooked breakfast and walk over 24 miles today in 8 hours. The roads are much quieter today, and I see some fantastic views that you would not see when driving in a car. I come across an amusingly relevant road name—'Long Walk' and enjoy a brief respite with coffee and two sausage rolls (treat time) at a café in Kings Langley.

My energy levels are boosted, and I switch footwear between my walking shoes and trainers. I come across an image in a roadside mirror showing a very dapper walker wearing a similar outfit to myself (he must also have been kitted out by Mick and Elaina at TrekHire UK), and funnily enough, he is also six feet tall. What a coincidence. I have a very enjoyable walk through Verulamium Park and enjoy finding out more about its history when I get online:

The Roman city of Verulamium

Shortly, after the second Roman invasion of Britain, Verulamium was established around the Iron Age settlement of Verlamion. The destruction of the settlement by Boudicca afforded the opportunity to implement Roman town planning principles, and Verulamium became one of the largest Roman cities in Britain (at least by area). Unlike many other Roman towns and cities, Verulamium's sub-surface remains were largely undisturbed until the nineteenth century, allowing modern archaeologists to map the layout more comprehensively than elsewhere. But much remains to be done, and work continues. (Source www.stalbanshistory*)*

In the park, there is an interesting tribute sign to Boudicca whom I also read up on.

Boudicca was the queen of the Iceni people of Eastern England and led a major uprising against occupying Roman forces. Boudicca was married to Prasutagus, ruler of the Iceni people of East Anglia. When the Romans conquered southern England in AD 43, they allowed Prasutagus to continue to rule. However, when Prasutagus died the Romans decided to rule the Iceni directly and confiscated the property of the leading tribesmen. They are also said to have stripped and flogged Boudicca and raped her daughters.

These actions exacerbated widespread resentment at Roman rule. In 60 or 61 AD, while the Roman governor Gaius Suetonius Paullinus was leading a campaign in North Wales, the Iceni rebelled. Members of other tribes joined them. Boudicca's warriors successfully defeated the Roman Ninth Legion and destroyed the capital of Roman Britain, then at Colchester. They went on to destroy London and Verulamium (St Albans). Thousands were killed.

Finally, Boudicca was defeated by a Roman army led by Paulinus. Many Britons were killed and Boudicca is thought to have poisoned herself to avoid capture. The site of the battle, and of Boudicca's death, are unknown.

(www.bbc.co.uk/history/historic_figures/boudicca)

It strikes me reading this how much names have evolved over time—not necessarily better or worse, simply different. How does that happen? I guess it is down to parents who want to be different but the first kids with different names will likely find their name a talking point! I do not recall there being a Prasutagus or Paullinus in any of my schools or workplaces—there will have been some Paul's however so maybe that is the modern-day equivalent of Paullinus. The first child named Apple or Amber—I wonder what they think of their name? Are they pleased to be 'unique' or would rather not have the attention?

St Albans city centre is quite busy on a lovely sunny day, it is several years since I have visited here with Anne, and we stayed at Sopwell House not too far away. We visited Sopwell House with three other couples before we had children and then subsequently once for Anne's birthday weekend when my parents would babysit enabling us to escape for a break. You will notice in the photos below; the photograph of the portable loo being towed away—I must confess that having taken advantage of the portaloo facility I only expected the owners to replenish the toilet roll—not remove the whole unit. It stimulates an amusing memory for me that makes me smirk as I walk along.

I was working in Mansfield at the time when I had a stomach cramp and dashed to the gent's toilet. I always check the toilet roll status before I sit down, and the first cubicle did not have any loo roll left just an empty holder—so I dashed into the next available cubicle. A couple of minutes later I heard somebody else enter the first cubicle—but they clearly did not have time to check the loo roll status. The door was locked, and the necessary toilet activity was underway. I am not sure if we had all eaten something dodgy at lunchtime. I really struggled with myself not to start laughing—which resulted in me making strange noises as the stifled guffaws just slipped out. The guy next door had no paper so the only option would have been for him to waddle from the cubicle with his trousers around his ankles as he looked for some spare loo roll sheets. Maybe in hindsight, I should have found a loo roll for him but once I had finished, I washed my hands and exited as quickly as I could. I never did discover who it was.

I arrive at the White Hart in Welwyn late afternoon, which is great as it gives me time to relax and refresh. The pub is generous in donating a lovely comfortable room to me (even though the pub itself is closed). My timing is not great in arriving on a Monday as the food looks nice on the menu but is obviously not available tonight—I will have to visit again another day. I improvise with my clothes washing as I want to ensure that my special merino wool socks are always available and utilise the rail outside the room to get the late afternoon sun.

Anne scares me when we talk on the phone, that a passer-by might take them, but in hindsight, it would need to be a very brave thief to consider stealing my now cleanish underwear or socks. In the meantime, I order a (way too large) Domino's pizza and have regretted it ever since as I get an almost daily text updating me on special pizza offers in Welwyn regardless of my location.

We get into a nice routine where I write a summary of the day's walk, send it to Anne who re-writes it so that it makes sense—and then posts along with multiple photos.

News Headlines Context, 14 September 2020

In news headlines, Germany is staring down the barrel of a £1.8billion (€2bn) black hole if there is no trade deal between the UK and European Union, business chiefs have admitted. Britons will be blasted by scorching highs of 32C this week as temperatures soar before high pressure—helped in part by warm air from tropical storm Paulette—could be nudged aside to allow low pressure and more turbulent conditions to 'become more dominant' across the UK.

Coronavirus Daily Context, 14 September 2020

The Coronavirus 'rule of six' comes into force in England today, meaning any social gatherings of more than six people will break the law. People face fines of up to £3,200 if they do not abide by the new measure, which applies to both indoor and outdoor settings and follows a rapid increase in the number of daily positive cases. Regulations enabling the enforcement of the rule were published late on Sunday night, around 30 minutes before they came into effect. More than 3,000 COVID-19 cases were recorded in the UK for the third day in a row on Sunday—the first time since May that cases were above 3,000 on three consecutive days.

"The virus is surging in many countries and some that had apparent success in suppressing initial outbreaks are also seeing infections rise once again. The World Health Organisation (WHO) has said Europe is likely to see an increase in COVID-19 cases over the next few months. The WHO's Europe director said: 'It's going to get tougher. In October and November, we are going to see more mortality'."

Tracking new cases 3,392; deaths 21
(source: coronavirus.data.gov.uk)

For me it feels like a parallel universe—the daily virus updates make depressing reading and yet as I walk up and down empty country lanes it feels unreal to me. Perhaps the reality will bite as I visit the busier locations.

Sunrise Chalfont.

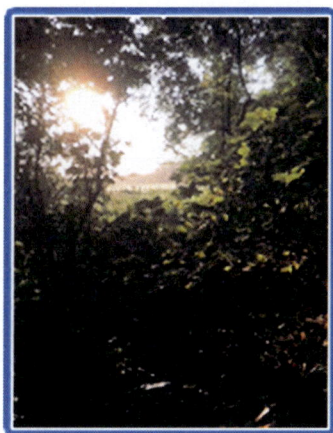

St Giles Philips Hill Wood.

Aptly named road sign.

Another 'cool' walker in the mirror—Saint Michael.

Saint Albans Cathedral.

Portable toilet.

Saint Albans DIY clothesline outside my room.

Day of Arrival at Milestone One

Day 3. Tuesday 15 September 2020

Today is the first day of the logistical challenge to move my 85-litre rucksack from one pitstop to the next without it being on my back or in Anne's car. Over the past two days, Anne has acted as my 'rucksack mule' transporting the heavyweight. Today the taxi arrives early (7:00 a.m.) and I take a photo of the number plate in case of foul play, it all worked out fine, but my running costs will add up to £40–50 per day at this rate. I am enjoying the freedom of the road and the fresh air. I am also taking advantage of the lovely weather, and whilst handwashing is not one of my favourite activities, I am going to try and wash my socks, shirts, and underwear every couple of days.

Particularly, the socks as they are key to helping me manage my feet. So, as you will see from the photographs, I am able to dry the gear quite effectively by tying the socks to the straps on my rucksack and then 'rotating' as the exposed sock area dries out. I looked cool (at least in my own mind) and perhaps the 'human drier' could become a new trend. I am really enjoying the sights. Today is a day of signs really.

Walking through Woolmer Green I see a whole array of amusing signs that somebody has spent a lot of time creating. For example, a sign with the face of a clock showing the hands at ten minutes past 10 o'clock with the caption 'This clock is correct twice a day'. Another that made me chuckle: question: 'How can you help a one-eyed sparrow?'

Answer: 'Take it to a Birds Eye shop'.

I also come across a strange sign with a 30-mile speed limit, this was not the strange part, but it instructed drivers to slow down as there are 'free-range children' around. I have seen this sign for eggs previously but never children. I am walking right next to a large windmill, and I am so close that I can touch it— in different times (i.e., pre-COVID) I would have taken a few minutes out to have a look inside, but unfortunately, it is closed.

Edwinstree school is in **Buntingford** in Hertfordshire—my first town reached with two specific locations as part of the first milestone—the first being the school. It is a middle school for 9-13-year-olds and is very much as I remember it, in fact, the coats of paint at the entrance do not appear to have changed in the last 40 years. I do a few takes of my 'milestone video', which Anne will then post on Facebook in the evening.

In 1976, I started Edwinstree school at the same time that we moved to a new house. I recall spending the night with Dad camping on the floor in a sleeping bag, which felt like a real adventure to me. I think I even had a beer or maybe it was shandy in those days (and I would have only been nine years old, so I hope so!) Either way, I felt very grown-up.

From there, it is only a 5-minute walk to White Hart Close where we lived in the late 1970s. Again, it is very much as I remember it although the current owners of the house have invested in a lovely solid wood exterior door. Having worked for a global door manufacturer I am able to appreciate the quality of this. I record my second video and manage to escape before anybody questions why a strange man with wet socks dangling from his rucksack is taking videos around the cul-de-sac. I walk past the outside of the health centre where we used to play football as children.

I distinctly recall as a child having a few spots emerge on my body that turned out to be chickenpox (several friends had already had this) but ensuring that I did not inform my mother until AFTER I had played football. Otherwise, I knew the consequence would be to stay indoors with immediate effect if I had told her. I cannot remember the football score. I do though, remember the secret alleyway connecting the residential area to the High Street at the back of the health centre and manage to find a coffee shop.

The waitress is exceedingly kind and donates her tips into my collection tin, and I set off for the final ten miles to Royston where I have a B&B booked for the evening. This part of the walk is not as pleasant as it is basically along the A10, a terribly busy road. It is fine when there is a pavement near the residential areas but walking either directly on the main road, or on the verges, is not pleasant when there are lorries thundering past a metre or two away.

As I am walking along, I recall other memories from my time in Buntingford. I chose this as my first milestone because we spent many years in the area and during the formative years for us three boys. I have generally followed the rules, I would say, I am certainly not a troublemaker; however, I do remember at primary school when I did break the rules. I am frequently told that I do not have a musical note in my body, but I was quite good at the recorder and somehow ended up in the top group.

I always preferred to read and enjoyed the classroom. I am not quite sure how I managed this, but the children were summoned to attend music classes by group, which meant a handful of individuals would leave and the remainder of the class would continue learning. I never left when my group was called. For weeks and months, I just did not attend—I am not sure how they did not have a register, but I am quite proud that I could continue to do what I preferred without being caught.

I also remember playing football for Buntingford Cougars. Both the team and I were awful, and I do pity my father who paced the touchline much as I did with my boys—minus any of the excitement or adrenaline or skill that I was able to witness. Poor dad with three boys of different ages he found 75% of his weekend had disappeared—although Tim and Andrew at least had some sporting talent to display.

My team would generally be on the wrong end of double-digit defeats, but I am sure that is where my perseverance and commitment traits were born. While I may not have been a natural sports superstar, I was OK academically. I do remember the weekly spelling test. If we did not learn them or scored badly then it was a detention. I remember sometimes forgetting to learn them but was good enough to 'wing it' sometimes and managed to avoid detention.

Looking back in time this was really the main period in my life when the adults and children were both neighbours and friends—in effect a community. We have had nice neighbours elsewhere but not like in White Hart Close where, as children we would play outside in the cul-de-sac, or in each other's houses, and the adults would meet socially. I recall our neighbours taking us out for a farewell meal just before we moved to Malvern. I was anti-moving as it would mean starting again, building new friendships—on the other hand, it took me out of my comfort zone, which is a good thing.

On the night of the farewell meal, I was a bit disgruntled. My appetite at the age of 12 was large, and I would eat more than mum for example. However, all the children were grouped together, and I had to eat from the children's menu— yes, the sausage and chips or fishfinger and chips with small portions; I was not amused. At least, I was not given the crayons and colouring in—that might have sent me into a meltdown.

I survive the A10 much as I did the ignominy of the small farewell meal and thanks very much to the Orchard House in Royston who kindly donate bed and breakfast to the cause. The only downside is that my feet are quite sore today red, itchy, and blistered to be specific and the location of the B&B is outside the town centre, so I end up walking a further (painful) mile in my flip flops to find dinner (Wetherspoons special tonight) before hobbling back to the B&B. I must confess to being concerned about my feet.

I realise I am putting them through a challenge however I am surprised at the redness, blisters, and general soreness that I am feeling. I am really worried although try to block it out because I have walked only around 70 miles and therefore still have over 530 miles to go, and I am literally hobbling towards the end of each day. I really could not face failing on this challenge—all the effort that has gone into it, the support I have had, and the funds being raised for good causes would all be for nothing. I will need to manage the situation.

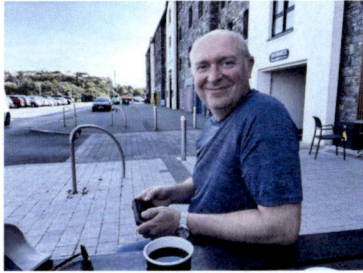

Andrew: I am calling David a couple of times a day, usually trying to time with the hope he might be stopping around 11am for a coffee, and then again later in the day. It seems a good routine to try and adopt, as I want to stay in touch and live the moments together, even though I am not there in person, I have also learned to use technology to overcome David's lack of geographical awareness (yes, I have decided by now it's not my lack of geography at fault. 😊 So, I have got him to accept my phone as a tracker, so at any time in the day can find where he is and what progress he is making.)

Daily News Context, 15 September 2020

In news headlines, European Commission officials will include Britain in a list of countries that can export food and agricultural products to the bloc once the new legislation is revealed. It comes after eurocrats warned firms could be blocked from sending British cheese, lamb, and beef into Northern Ireland after the end of the post-Brexit transition period. They told industry chiefs the ban was unavoidable unless the Government published its plans for food and plant safety by the end of October.

Coronavirus Daily Context, 15 September 2020

"China claims to have created a successful coronavirus vaccine that may be ready for the general public in November. None of the vaccines currently developed by China has passed the third stage clinical trials. However, Beijing said Phase 3 clinical trials were proceeding smoothly and the vaccines could be ready for the general public come November. Coronavirus breakthrough: British hospital patients to test antibody cocktail. At least 176 hospitals across the country will be taking part in the new recovery trial by the University of Oxford, who was responsible for discovering the steroid dexamethasone can help save lives."
Tracking new cases 3,552; deaths 18
(source: coronavirus.data.gov.uk)

More encouraging updates today with apparent progress in China and the UK on potential vaccines—good news! I am hoping that I can complete my planned walk—it is weird to have a plan, which I can control with regard to miles, rests, stops and yet all around me is this weird environment that I cannot control and where the rate of infections and deaths continues to increase rapidly.

Taxi taking my rucksack.

Human clothes drier.

Beautiful sunrise in Welwyn.

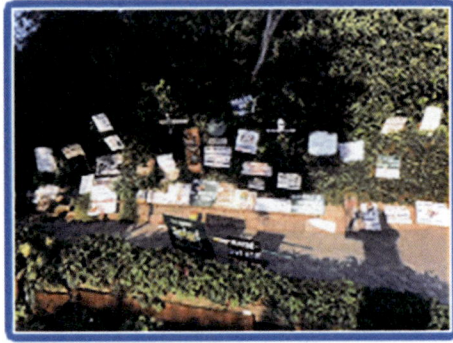

Great array of signs—Woolmer Green.

Unique sign Ardeley.

Cromer Windmill—Ardeley—Cromer.

Me at Edwinstree school Buntingford.

Me in White Hart Close.

Twelve Days Before Arriving at Milestone Two

Day 4. Wednesday 16 September 2020, Royston to Huntingdon

I get up to an early start and a healthy continental breakfast to take away with me; the sun continues to shine. I am walking 21.54 miles (approximately!) from Royston to Huntingdon today and it's amusing to see some of the local village names—where do these names originate from? For example, I walk through a village called 'Bassingbourn cum Kneesworth'—who comes up with that name? who then approves it? and then assuming the signwriter is paid per letter then this is clearly an attractive sign job compared to Ely for example. I am truly clear in my mind that the smaller lanes and bridleways are so much more pleasant to walk on than the A roads.

It is so peaceful with the sun shining, very few people around and just the sound of my walking shoes treading on the path (along with the squishing of my blisters squeezing against the shoes). I have around five or six blisters now, and they tend to mirror the same places on my left and right feet. For example, I have a blister on the end of my fourth toe on each foot. Blisters are a real nuisance.

It reminds me of the story of the princess and the pea when the princess could feel the pea all the way through her mattress and sheets. Well, the blisters I have are a similar shape to a pea—or perhaps more of a brussels sprout—but the pain that such small blisters can inflict is hugely disproportionate to their size! I am never sure whether I should actively pop them or wait for nature to take its course. One of Anne's nurse friends advises me through Anne to leave them alone as they could become infected; Andrew advises me to take a needle, 'burn it and pop'. I follow the nurse's advice.

I manage to find a nice coffee shop in Papworth Everard where the owner generously donates 3 beers for me to have as refreshment at later date—very generous with the only downside being that I need to magically conjure up some space, put them in my rucksack and carry them. Still, I can always find room for beer. More blisters are emerging, and my feet are also quite red/hot today, so I look for a pharmacy—unfortunately, it is closed for lunch. A lady overhears me in the café explaining what I am doing and that I need a pharmacy—she kindly donates £5 into my collection tin and fortunately once again it is a note, not coins.

There is a funny moment when I am walking near a school and the pupils are leaving the school for the day at the point that I walk past. I overhear one young schoolgirl asking her mother why is that man walking with ski poles? I did not catch the answer, which is probably a good thing.

It is a great feeling again to see the sign for Sandford House—the Wetherspoon in Huntingdon. The manager has got permission to donate a room for the night, and it is a lovely room with a comfortable big bed to stretch out on. This is important as I am just over six feet tall and need space to stretch out. It is quite satisfying being the tallest adult in the family.

Matthew and James are maybe an inch smaller than me (which is clearly important psychologically when I need to assert myself). Andrew used to be the same height as me until his hair disappeared. Tim is a couple of inches shorter—so rationally he cannot be classified as small, however, he is the smallest and therefore the butt of any heightism jokes—and there are always plenty of those. Ironically, his son Will has shot up in recent years and is now taller than me—so on average they are in the right height zone—see there is another dig (I just cannot resist).

I hobble into a Boots chemist not far from the hotel and the pharmacist recommends a cream that really helps reduce the redness/itchiness on my feet when I apply it. I need to call in the help of the 'support team' (James this time) during the evening as the unlimited data package that I have purchased for use on the second mobile phone (James's spare phone) has expired after only 4 days. This is not good as I use this phone for Google Maps, and without that, I have no idea where I am going. James checks into it, and I must have been mis-sold the original deal—nevertheless he is able to go online and renew a truly unlimited data package for 30 days. You see it really is a team effort.

> Andrew: The language David was using by now was different to his usual conversation and his normal optimistic and buoyant tomfoolery was waning. It was clear that he was concerned about the state of his feet. Moreover, some signs of frustration that his feet were causing issue. I also had the task of swapping my tracker from his old phone to the new one because he was using Maps with it now that James had unlocked the data issue. I was still in the habit of calling quite often and found the timing best if I clashed with him trying to use the map on the phone at the same time as me calling.

News Headlines Context, 16 September 2020

In news headlines, the Foreign Secretary said talks with the US have been progressing well and vowed the multi-billion pound tie-up would provide a 'huge opportunity' for jobs and businesses in the UK. The boost comes just days after the UK tied up a bumper trade agreement with Japan worth £15 billion. Boris Johnson said the UK-Japan deal will provide a springboard for Britain to be at the forefront of a renaissance in global trade.

Coronavirus Daily Context, 16 September 2020

North-east faces local lockdown restrictions on Friday as cases spike—curfew expected. Boris Johnson will introduce local lockdown restrictions across the north-east of England this week. The areas expected to be governed by the new restrictions include Newcastle, Northumberland, North Tyneside, South Tyneside, Gateshead, Country Durham and Sunderland. The new rule will come into effect from Friday morning, which could force pubs, restaurants and other licensed premises to close from 10:00 p.m. each day, as a curfew is introduced.

"But the hospitality venues will be allowed to reopen, unlike in Bolton where pubs and restaurants are takeaway only. Residents of the areas will also be banned from socialising with anyone from a different household. The huge area of Rhondda Cynon Taf in South Wales is being forced into lockdown following a surge in coronavirus cases, the country's Government has announced."

Tracking new cases 4,367; deaths 26
(source: coronavirus.data.gov.uk)

This means I will have to arrive in daylight hours as I head Northwards and consume my pint of beer before 10:00 p.m. Fortunately, Wales is not on this trek. However, I am heading into the Northeast and am staying in a mix of hotels, pubs and bed and breakfasts so it's worrying that some venues could be forced to close. It feels like one step forwards in that I am making good progress and yet potentially it could be two steps back if I cannot stay where planned.

Bassingbourn Cum Kneesworth.

Great name for a village.

Kneesworth

3 beers kindly donated.

Eleven Days Before Arriving at Milestone Two

Day 5. Thursday 17 September 2020, Huntingdon to Stibbington

Today I break through the 100-mile barrier …. Only 500 to go! I am walking nearly 23 miles from Huntingdon to the Sibson Inn in Stibbington near Peterborough. The mornings are better for me, and I walk faster than I do in the afternoons, although I have noticed my walking pace is dropping every day (well under 3 miles per hour now).

Last night was a bit chillier so before setting off I re-zip the bottoms of my trousers back on. It works for 30 minutes until the sun comes out, and it is hot again, whereupon the rucksack comes off and the trouser bottoms are carried not worn. My feet seem to be getting worse each day, but I have a rest day approaching, which I will spend with them raised above my head so that the blood can flow to my other body parts.

I am still learning how best to use the maps on one phone, with mileage tracking working on the other and the portable charger in my bum bag—wires are everywhere. It is ironic that I am inept really with technology—particularly as in my last few roles I have had responsibility for the websites and digital marketing. I know what is needed and how to get results, but I usually have an expert working for me who can make things happen, and if I do not then I hire one. I think that is also a sign of somebody in the right role when they can bring in and coach or harness the experts with key skills to raise the performance of the whole team.

I reflect a lot today on what I want to do next. I have enjoyed myself most in the roles where I have led a team that I enjoy working with and can coach to improve—and where I work with peers that I trust and enjoy working with, usually delivering great results. So my roles at Black & Decker and Jewson stand out for me in that regard. When I think back most of my jobs have been working for larger companies with revenue £1 billion or more and overall, I have enjoyed myself, I have learned a lot and continue to learn but at the same time I am always a 'cog in a much larger wheel'.

Some of my ex-colleagues have become the captain of smaller businesses and that does appeal to me. My view is that I have evolved into a 'marketing leader' albeit that was not my intention when I left university in 1988. A good friend of mine, Simon, recently summed up his views of me from our time working together at Jewson. I might even try and sign him up as my agent! His views were that I am a blend of different roles of which marketing is only a part.

When I left Jewson, I recall my boss at the time in my farewell speech referring to my role as the 'David Fenton role' because I had grabbed over time different elements such as customer experience, the specialist businesses such as tool hire and showrooms, and digital marketing for the larger Saint Gobain group (not just Jewson)—and effectively built it into a larger role. Looking from the outside-in, Simon sees what I have delivered covering initiatives from sales, marketing, strategy, and trading.

I think Simon is right. I am not a pure or classical marketer. I enjoy variety and do not like to be put in a box. I am quite tenacious—it all starts with having a plan and then executing the plan. However, I have yet to see a plan that does not evolve, and I have never seen a plan implemented 100% because things change, and assumptions are never perfect. For me, that is where the challenge and the fun come in—I keep the customer and the original objectives at the heart of the project but then I must adapt to new information or unforeseen issues.

One of the things I have developed over the years is that I work with all functions to make things happen and so I have a good understanding of finance, supply chain, operations, and sales. I like the potential career route of business consulting although it is not always easy to get the right assignments. It is a contacts game, and my approach has been to build up my quality contacts versus chasing for the quantity. Not sure if that is the right approach for consulting or not. So, either route appeals—working in a smaller company where I can be a bigger fish or consulting where I can control my day and my projects (assuming there is the demand for my services). I am clear though that I do not want to return to a large corporate role.

I do not have any technological experts with me today on my walk so for my destination I insert the Google Maps postcode (later to learn it is best to put the hotel name as the destination). The route map consequently takes me to a farmhouse rather than the hotel—fortunately, the owner explains I am only about 30 mins away although the hotel itself is situated on the A1, so I must walk a couple of hundred yards up the A1. Horrible.

The traffic is a constant flow of small, medium, and large vehicles but it is the HGVs that are the worst, and I get tooted at frequently. I can feel the air vibrations in the small gap between me walking on the verge and the big trucks careering past me. No wonder I cannot recall seeing pedestrians on dual carriageways previously.

Once in my room, I phone the 'support team' as the next day is supposedly 17.5 miles walking up the A1 which I do not fancy. The team come up with a good idea to get a taxi to the next location and then walk the required miles around that location—so that is what I do. The food at the Sibson Inn is lovely, and I go for 3 courses—prawns, Dover sole and apple cake—that is the good thing in walking 20 miles a day I do not have to think about calories....

News Headlines Context, 17 September 2020

In news headlines, the WHO has said it would not reduce its two-week recommendations for self-isolation after several European nations slashed the amount of time individuals are required to quarantine. In the UK, anyone who has come into contact with a person diagnosed with COVID-19 must cut themselves off from the outside world for 10 days.

Coronavirus Daily Context, 17 September 2020

'Wake up!' WHO criticises the UK coronavirus strategy and warns infection rate is 'alarming.'

"The UK Government has been ordered to get tough on its quarantine measures for people known to have been exposed to coronavirus, as new cases soar across the continent. A major announcement from Health Secretary Matt Hancock is expected this morning. The new restrictions will include a curfew of 10:00 p.m. for pubs and restaurants. People will also be unable to socialise with anyone outside their household."

Tracking new cases 4,632; deaths 27
(source: coronavirus.data.gov.uk*)*

Fingers crossed I do not come into contact with somebody who has the virus as two weeks of self-isolation would really mess up my schedule. I find myself dreading a phone or call or text from one of the places that I have stayed telling me there has been an infection at their premises and that I need to self-isolate; the positive thinking that I clutch at is that many people are not travelling and so the occupancy rates are extremely low.

Nice kick-off to the day.

Display Aeroplane.

Dinner.
Glatton Dover sole—with strategically placed collection tin!

Ten Days Before Arriving at Milestone Two

Day 6. Friday 18 September 2020, Walk Around South Witham Area.

It feels very strange getting in a taxi this morning. We drive to the Travelodge also on the A1 at South Witham, Grantham where I drop my bag and follow a route locally. My feet are painful, and I make a mistake in thinking fresh air would be good to 'air' my hot, swollen feet so I walk in flip-flops. The first few miles are OK, but after a while, the Compeed plasters are sticking to my flip flops and my feet—joining the feet and flip tops together into one long string—so that in effect I cannot easily take my flip flops off.

My big toe on my right foot is sore, swollen and bruised, and I have multiple blisters—not good. My feet are red and throbbing and the cream I got earlier in the week seems to have stopped working. I have a rest day approaching but walking in flip-flops is not sustainable. I walk the 17 miles and again there are some nice views although I am perhaps not in the right physical or emotional state to relish them; I am close to Melton and am briefly tempted to walk a little further to enjoy the infamous pork pie experience.

The end of the day is the worst part of my walking experience to date. I misjudge where to join the A1 to return to the Travelodge joining at North Wisham and not South Wisham and must walk 0.9 miles up the A1 in flip flops. I kind of 'Wisham' that I had not made that mistake. Lorries speeding past and often flashing me with their headlights is not fun. In theory, a pedestrian can walk on the A1 but, it is not safe—it was such a good call NOT to walk 17 miles up the A1.

Jelly babies are a godsend, and I am incredibly grateful to Anne as they would never have been on my provisions list. I work out where best to locate them in my rucksack for easy access and undoubtedly the black and orange ones are the tastiest. It is a tough call to decide whether to suck or chew, but it is exceedingly difficult to control—I start sucking but there is always an involuntary point where my gnashers start chomping and the jelly babies have been consumed.

My feet are not in a good way; however, I have the upside of the 3 beers that I had been donated earlier in the week along with a pizza that I will order to be delivered to the hotel. The hotel kindly stores them in their fridge so I can have them cold. I struggle to get down the stairs as each step downwards jars the feet. I am effectively shuffling my way up and down. I feel some relief lying out on the bed with a cool beer in my grasp.

Every Friday we have a Fenton facetime call with my parents and brothers where we catch up on the latest news. I am pressured into 'showing my feet' and the reaction of my mother 'Oh, David' in that maternal tone when I show them, makes me think again about the state they are in. I have seen them deteriorate each and every day but the reaction of mum seeing them for the first time makes me worry. What if I am creating permanent damage here? I do not understand why they are so sore but assume it is a combination of the constant pounding, the stupid mistake I made on day one, and the heat.

The walking shoes themselves feel amazingly comfortable—they do not rub or chafe—it is just the feet inside the shoes that are my problem. The next day I am planning to walk to Newark, but on reflection, during the night, I think I had better cut my losses and take a break to let my feet repair. I discuss this with Anne in the early hours of the next day and decide to pause the walk temporarily and very reluctantly decide to return home to recuperate.

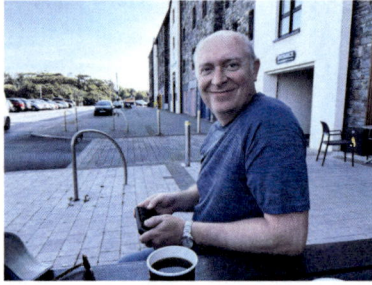

Andrew: This was a definite low for David, the frustrations that his feet will not match what his drive and determination need. It was an awkward Friday Facetime as the dawn of realization fully landed that those plans needed to change. The various encouraging options of what else can now happen were well received by David but the realization of halting the plans were definitely the prime focus of his attention.

> Mum and Dad: Although David had mentioned he was struggling with his feet It was such a shock to see them on the screen. We could not believe and when he said he could not face going out for something to eat we knew it was really serious. So relieved when he decided to take some time out.

News Headlines Context, 18 September 2020

In news headlines, US Democratic nominee Joe Biden has been ordered to retract his threats over a UK–US trade deal, after he warned there would be no such pact if Boris Johnson's form of Brexit harmed the Good Friday Agreement. Cornwall mining boom: the UK set for a surge in mining after 'significant' lithium discovery and could receive a major jobs boost after a local mining firm announced the discovery of lithium in the county. The metal—a key component in electric car batteries—was found in deep underground hot springs just north of the town of Redruth. Cornish Lithium said it was of a 'globally significant' grade and could be enough to meet all the UK's demand if and when the country moves from fossil fuel vehicles to electric ones.

Coronavirus Daily Context, 18 September 2020

"The UK has barely a fortnight to act before COVID-19 spirals out of control, a group of independent scientists has warned, unveiling a 10-point plan, which they said could save thousands of lives—with a second wave inevitable if

nothing is done. The latest COVID-19 figures for England and Wales comes as the Government confirmed local lockdown restrictions will be enforced across parts of the North West, Midlands and West Yorkshire to 'curb rising infection rates'. On Tuesday, residents of Merseyside, Warrington, Halton and Lancashire (with the exception of Blackpool and Greater Manchester) will be subject to additional lockdown restrictions. This includes not socialising with people from outside of households and supporting bubbles inside. A curfew on restaurants, pubs and other premises will also be implemented between 10:00 p.m. and 5:00 a.m."

Tracking new cases 4,957; deaths 23
(source: coronavirus.data.gov.uk)

The virus seems to be like a tidal wave in gathering momentum—I am hoping Greater Manchester as one of my travel zones can remain at a low rate for the next couple of weeks at least. Unfortunately, with the decision, I have made tonight I will be travelling southwards not north. I have no idea what this means about my schedule and when I can start again.

I need to cancel all the bookings I have made. I feel incredibly low, which is probably compounded by the highs that I have been feeling up until now, from the walk itself and reaching all the destinations as planned so far. It is so frustrating, and I feel so helpless. I just hope this is not terminal.

South Witham.

South Witham Re-joining the A1.

North Witham—horrible walk!

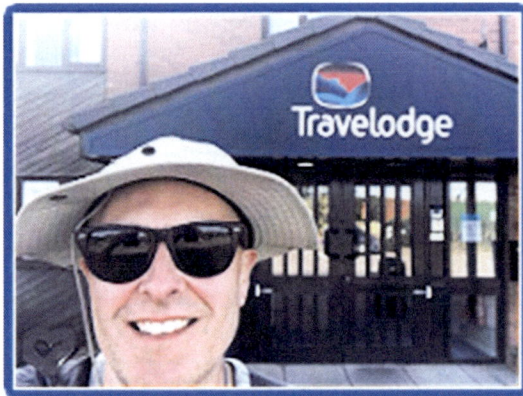

Return to Travelodge South Witham.

Photos of Day 6

Day 7. Saturday 19 September 2020—Day 21, Sunday, 4 October—Feet
Repair Time

In the morning, I cancel my hotel for Newark, organise a taxi to the train station and get the train from Grantham to Wokingham via London. I then start the process of deferring all my future stays as in my head I plan for around a week recovery albeit my medical diagnosis skills are not a real strength. I still feel really frustrated as my legs, my fitness generally is all good, but my annoying feet are the issue and after only 6 days I am back home and who knows for how long. It is rationally the right decision but that does not make me feel any better whatsoever.

I speak to a doctor over the phone about my big toe specifically as the bruising is severe—he diagnoses gout. This is then backed up by the local doctor. Anne buys some cherry pills to help but the reality is that it is not gout. I manage at the end of the first week resting to see a podiatrist who diagnoses it as just bad bruising and bad blisters. On reflection, I think I walked too many miles per day, day after day, and in hot weather so my feet were overheated in the boots— reminding me of the bright pink gammon steaks when they emerge from the slow cooker.

A combination of soaking my feet in Epsom salts, using ice on the bruising and time itself helps the feet to slowly repair. But by the end of the first week of recuperating, I am still not ready as there is still pain, so I end up taking 2 weeks out in total. I find the whole period very frustrating as the nice weather starts to disappear. I spend my time replanning the remainder of my route—multiple phone calls to hotels and B&B's.

Also, I am following strong advice from the 'support team' as I reduce the miles per day down to 15-20 compared to my original 20-30, and plan in more regular rest days. So, it will take me longer to complete the walk, but it will 'hopefully' be achievable.

James: "When I picked Dad up from the station after he had probably overestimated the difficulty of walking such long distances for 6 days in a row, I could tell he was frustrated and wanting to just get back on the road. Sitting around doing nothing at home is not really his cup of tea, I wonder where I get it from?..."

> Matthew: I remember when Dad had to come home around the end of September. You could tell how much pain he was in by the way he hobbled around the house. I remember wanting to help him as a much as I could and help him replan his routes, but I also had my first two professional exams coming up. You could see him getting frustrated by this forced break, but he definitely needed it.

News Headlines Context, 19 September 2020

In news headlines, The EU has been told by German politicians to prepare for a no-deal Brexit outcome with the UK, with one warning: "We must not allow ourselves to be blackmailed." Boris Johnson is proceeding with the UK Government's Internal Market Bill, which would look to override key elements of the Withdrawal Agreement signed with the EU last year and consequently, break international law. Chaos in London where thousands gathered in Trafalgar Square in FURIOUS lockdown protest—police arrest 32.

ANTI-LOCKDOWN protesters have scuffled with police today in Trafalgar square amid fury over a possible return to lockdown as the nation braces itself for the second wave of coronavirus—with police making 32 arrests.

Coronavirus Daily, 19 September 2020

"Ministers are thought to be considering a two-week 'circuit break' in a bid to slow transmission of the virus. The Prime Minister continues to insist a second national lockdown is the 'last thing anybody wants' but has admitted the current coronavirus measures would need to be kept 'under review'. He has however warned the UK is facing a second wave of coronavirus."

Tracking new cases 4,855; deaths 20

(source coronavirus.data.gov.uk)

A second national lockdown would be another major blow for me on top of my healing time out. It feels as if I am lying helplessly on a beach on a very windy day as the waves of doom wash over me and stop me from getting a tan. Some of the waves are of my own making—I cannot get away from the fact that they are my feet! Some of the waves are out of my control—I cannot control the virus or lockdown. I need to navigate the waves wherever they come from using my super surfboard and be flexible enough to handle the different sized waves that try to knock me down or catch me unawares.

Train at Newark station.

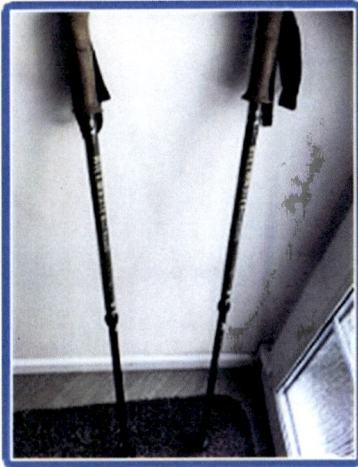

Walking Poles–temporarily parked

Walking shoes and Boots–time for them to "air"

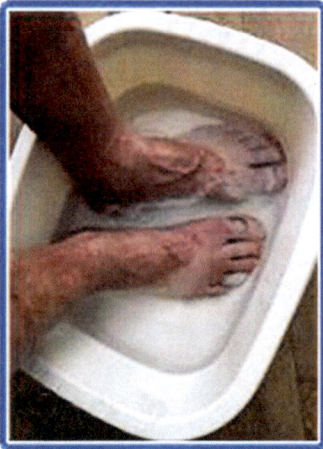
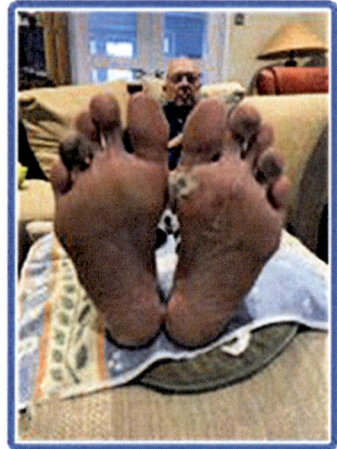

State of my feet

Date	Activity	Mood
20 September 2020	*Not a lot of activity—I sit on the sofa with feet raised. I do get well looked after and have photographs taken of my feet. I am targeting a week out to recuperate, and I plan to start again next weekend (ish). Nice Chinese takeaway.*	
21 September 2020	*Having spoken to the doctor over the phone, I have a physical check-up. This supports the gout diagnosis. I sit on the sofa with my feet raised. I also enjoy driving a car again—it's the small things sometimes……I cancel imminent hotel/B&B visits and highlight that I will contact them again when ready.*	

22 September 2020	Bored	
23 September 2020	Bored	
24 September 2020	*Blisters are healing but the big right toe is still very sore. I visit a nearby chiropodist to get further advice. The chiropodist is very friendly. We end up with a win-win where her fee is kindly donated to the charity fund whilst I purchase a support sock that I do not need. Diagnosis is that it is not gout but bruising …….*	
25 September 2020	*I am mobile and able to walk short distances. I actually enjoyed going to Waitrose and doing the shop today. No chance I am ready to go this weekend though.*	

26 September 2020	Watching Netflix, reading books	😠
27 September 2020	Watching Netflix and contacting additional sponsors—to no avail	😠
28 September 2021	I am planning to go next weekend so started re-planning my route and working out distances, rest days etc	😄
29 September 2020	Contacting places to stay and then adjusting my route accordingly. It is nice to have a purpose and a plan of action	😄
30 September 2020	Bored	😠

1 October 2020	Bored	😠
2 October 2020	Repacking and leaving more kit behind. My feet are healing nicely.	😄
3 October 2020	The trek part 2 is definitely on and we have a lovely barbeque with Lisa and Simon.	😁
4 October 2020	I am ready	WOO HOO! 🤩

Eight Days Before Arriving at Milestone Two

Day 22. Monday 5 October, Newark to Laxton

I am extremely excited to be back on the roads—or hopefully pavements. There is some risk as I can feel discomfort on the big right toe, but my blisters are in much better shape and the skin is hardening. I have wasted or perhaps I should say 'invested' in two weeks recovery. Anne drops me at Wokingham train station, and I get the train to Newark via Waterloo and Kings Cross.

I take advantage of the time available to have a quick coffee and sandwich while waiting for my connection. I plan a relatively gentle start back as most of the morning is spent commuting and, I need to ease my way back rather than my typical full-on approach. The walk per day will be generally shorter than during the first week, and I also have more rest days scheduled so part of me is confident I can do this, part of me is still worried about managing my feet.

I come across both sides of the spectrum regarding sustainable living on my walk today. As you can see from the photos below there are clouds of smoke coming from the chimneys in the industrial area, is that good for the environment? On the other hand, I walk past a wind turbine, which appears to be a much more sustainable process to generate energy. I do not class myself as an eco-warrior, but I am very keen to do my bit and more, with regard to improving the environment. We are guardians of the planet and all that lives on it—it is our children or our children's children who inherit the legacy of what we leave behind.

If people think more along those lines, then I am sure the right behaviours will accelerate. There has been significant progress in recent years with regard to the removal of single-use plastic, a 95% reduction in the use of plastic bags for shopping since the five pence charge was introduced, and the recycling of waste materials but there is still a long way to go. On most of my days walking,

I have come across rubbish-strewn at the side of the road—litter, plastic bags, fishing weights of all things, and I guess this is a sign of the times—single-use face masks. It saddens me to see this and even more when I come across fly-tipping at the roadside.

I have recently read that the UK wants to lead the way in the generation of renewables—and more specifically, wind farms so I read up on the topic and discover a few interesting facts:

Wind power is the most significant generator of renewable energy in the UK. The onshore and offshore wind farms produced 14.8% of all electricity consumed by UK homes and businesses in 2017. The turbines we use today are advanced technology based on the traditional windmill concept.

The UK has an enviable geographic position for the turbines that harness the winds' energy because of the high proportion of wind that's blown around and over the country in Europe. Although the initial investment is high, this renewable energy source produces no carbon emissions and is one of the safest and cleanest methods of generating electricity.

Wind Turbines

The bulk of the installations for UK use are offshore to the North of Scotland rather than the smaller less powerful land-based versions. The advantages of building these engineering projects at sea include aesthetics, costs, the ability to harness stronger wind speeds and superior electricity generation due to their sheer size.

Contrast that with the small farms built on land like those in Cornwall and you can see why more capacity gets constructed at sea. There are additional health and safety issues to overcome so the blade length is shorter and less powerful. The majority of the land that gets used is green belt and protected so is more difficult to gain planning permission.

Once installed, the blades quietly go about their business producing electricity with no pollution from carbon emissions.

Did you Know?

Wind Farm Facts for the UK The Cost of Electricity Produced

Fact 1: Offshore wind cost £120/MWh in 2018 with new installations forecasting a lower cost of £58/MWh (5.8 p/kWh) in 2022.

Fact 2: Onshore wind costs just £65/MWh now and is forecasted at £46/MWh in 2022 (4.6 p/kWh). The amount of electricity produced.

Fact 3: Wind energy generates 14.8% of all electricity in the UK.

Fact 4: The largest onshore wind farm is in Whitelee, Scotland with 215 Siemens wind turbines and a capacity of 539 MW. The Hornsea Project Two installation due for completion in 2022 will become the world's largest wind farm with a capacity of 1,386 megawatts that could power up to 1.3 million homes.

Fact 5: During a typical year, a turbine only operates at between 28% (onshore) and 39% (offshore) of its maximum capacity. There is less energy produced during the summer months when the wind speed becomes lower or negligible.

Fact 6: 40% of all wind energy generated over Europe blows over the UK.

Fact 7: The wind turbine drives a generator as the rotor blades (or arms) spin producing AC electricity from magnets moving over stationary wire coils. This energy gets converted into DC electricity to store in batteries or fed directly into the National Grid to satisfy power demand.

Wind Turbine Installations Around the UK

Fact 8: The average life of a wind turbine is 20 to 25 years.

Fact 9: There are 1,516 onshore UK wind projects with 7,047 turbines connected to the National Grid. Fact 10: There are 32 offshore UK wind farms with 1,716 turbines connected to the National Grid.

Source: ww.businesselectricityprices.org.uk/wind-turbine-facts/

I like the idea of potentially working in the arena of sustainability and contributing to the plan to achieve the carbon-neutral targets. I am by no means an expert on the topic, but I do think that this is one of three 'mega life topics' where we can improve the life quality for future generations—along with space exploration and helping the less well-off regions/communities.

I am looking forward to visiting Laxton where Sam the owner of the hotel generously donates a room and continental breakfast. The Dovecote Inn at

Laxton is closed today (Sam mentioned he is filming; I am not sure what) but they have left a key to one of the rooms for me, (the bedrooms are located in a barn conversion next to the car park with a private entrance, original beams, and views over the barn's garden), which is both incredibly kind and very trusting. There are some lovely views on my walk today and Laxton itself is an attractive village seemingly full of character.

I particularly like the photograph below of the solitary cow standing on the horizon balanced with a bright green field underneath and a blue/white cloudy sky above—it is a photo of contrasts and solitude. The weather has turned a bit as I arrive in Laxton but I locate the Dovecote Inn with no problem. The cleaning lady for the premises is nearby and directs me where to go.

The room is lovely, the heat is on, and the bed is comfortable. Sam has kindly left breakfast for me with milk and butter in a little fridge. On the final stretch of the journey today, I buy some picnic items—sandwich, quiche, pork pie so I can have a lovely feast while reading my book.

I am back on the road, and it feels fantastic. My feet feel fine and certainly no deterioration although I realise it has only been a 'half-day at the office…'

News Headlines Context, 5 October 2020

In news headlines, panic has spread across Edinburgh tonight after a huge blaze erupted at a chemical plant near Scotland's capital. On social media, worried residents shared pictures showing the huge orange blaze in the night sky. Such was the power of the blaze, residents in Edinburgh could see the firelight up the sky although the plant is located in Fife.

Donald Trump to leave hospital as he declares COVID 'nothing to be afraid of' and he feels 'better than I did 20 years ago'. MICHEL Barnier will hold crunch talks with European coastal states after Boris Johnson warned EU vessels would be locked out of British waters without a Brexit pact.

Coronavirus Daily Context, 5 October 2020

"MPs have demanded the Prime Minister give them a vote on coronavirus measures going forward. On Tuesday, they will get a vote on the 'rule of six' which halts gatherings of more than six people—inside and outside. The Prime Minister's official spokesperson urged Tory MPs to back the motion, telling

reporters: *'Parliament has supported the measures, which we have put in place so far in the fight against coronavirus and we would urge MPs to continue to do so'.*"

Tracking new cases 16,555; deaths 70
(source: coronavirus.data.gov.uk)

Unfortunately, while I am back—the virus has not gone away and shows no signs of doing so. When I started my practice walks the rate of infection was between one and two thousand a day—it is now nearly seventeen thousand. The death rate in August could be counted on the fingers of one hand—I now need fourteen hands.

Noticeably quiet Wokingham train.

Kings Cross Station.

Setting off from Newark station.

Newark on Trent.

Very brown river.

Pollution in Newark Kelham.

Wind turbine—Bathley.

Tree shape caught my attention.

Food kindly left in the room by Sam

Very comfortable bed and room

Seven Days Before Arriving at Milestone Two

Day 23. Tuesday 6 October, Laxton to Morton

Today is a morale boost for me as I break the 150-mile barrier for the walk. It means I have now walked over 25% of my target (which sounds much better in my head than 75% of the walk is still ahead of me). Some lovely views again today, which is a major plus for me and always lifts my spirits; the downside is that walking through the small villages there are rarely any coffee shops available—particularly around 11:00–11:30 a.m. at the time when I start to suffer caffeine withdrawal symptoms.

It is also mixed bag weather-wise. I put on my sunscreen and shades and shortly after setting off, the rain cover is on my backpack and my waterproofs are on. I have seen several red telephone boxes in villages that have been converted to defibrillator storage boxes—a great idea and every village should have one.

In some ways, it is quite refreshing and easier walking in the rain, rather than with the intense heat of my first week—my feet are less hot and less 'gammon like' as a result. I know that I am meeting up with Anne after a few days, so I am managing with minimal supplies and the day rucksack. Anne will then bring the larger rucksack when we meet—the benefit is I do not have to plan—or fund—taxis to move the 85-litre rucksack between locations.

I have been incredibly lucky that Anne has been so supportive of this project. Not only indulging me to do it and disappear for a few weeks while incurring various costs to do the walk, but also spending time every day to help with the social media and coming out to visit on a couple of the legs. We have been married nearly 25 years now (oh dear that sounds like the next anniversary is a biggie and may need some funding) and we are quite different but perhaps that is what makes us click. Anne used to be a full-time teacher and still teaches on a supply basis, but she follows her real passion now, which is running her skincare, cleaning products and wellbeing businesses. I am immensely proud of how she has achieved this.

Anne is an ambassador with Tropic Skincare and I think she is still passionate about this—the business was started by Susie Ma who was a runner up on The Apprentice and Alan Sugar was so impressed that he invested and is now a 50/50 partner. As the award-winning products are natural the business fits nicely into Anne's natural, toxic free philosophy which includes refillable eco-friendly cleaning products, reducing the use of chemicals in the home. The businesses are complementary, and Anne has really developed her marketing and social media skills to good effect.

Anne is very much a people person and has great interpersonal skills so she can build and develop her network and engage with friends simultaneously. This is one of the areas we differ—Anne thrives on people interaction, whereas I have a much smaller network of close family and friends. I enjoy being with people, for example, at work and particularly to be with my marketing team when we are doing well business-wise, but I am equally happy on this walk where I am largely on my own. It means I can do what I want when I want.

I am relishing the peace and quiet, the start of the day when I can catch up on the news and sport as I have my breakfast and then again at the end of the day when I can indulge in a couple of pints and read my book. Anne is very caring and loving and would do anything for other people. It is funny when I think through our similarities and differences as I think the latter outnumber the former. Our similarities would cover our love for family and friends, we like a nice holiday, we like some comedy/period films and series, but this category largely falls into our 'differences'.

Regarding differences, I prefer sci-fi and action thriller films whereas Anne is more into the Rom-Com or drama category. I like a tidy, minimalistic approach to the house and its contents, Anne has many things and finds it hard to get rid of them. Ultimately though we acknowledge our differences and give each other space to do our own thing. It reminds me of something Uncle Kevin (the boys' uncle) once told me—you need to create space in your life to cover the key relationships.

You need one on one time with your spouse, you need to create time as a family, you need time alone with your children and you need time where you can be by yourself. I have found that to be very prophetic and for the majority of this walk I will be in the zone of time to myself.

I did cause some further angst to the 'support team' today. I should have made this decision while I was on my 'feet repair' break so I can add this to the list of errors I have made. The large rucksack that I am borrowing from Matthew was from his Duke of Edinburgh expeditions and has also been used during his exploration travels in the Far East the previous summer. One of the structural support poles at the rear of the rucksack has worn away the fabric and keeps coming away from the material and falling out of the canvas.

I had followed Matthew's technique and used Gaffa tape to repair this, however, this repeatedly comes off. I phone Mick and Elaina to see if I can borrow a larger rucksack—I later find out that they did not have one, and they end up loaning me a new one. Anne has basically to drive over today, collect it and then bring it up when we connect on Wednesday near Doncaster. As I said, I should have sorted this before—it is all a good learning experience as I told the 'support team'.

I am grateful to the Barns Country Guesthouse in Morton. Like most B&Bs they are struggling with the impact and consequences of the coronavirus but have still supported me by donating a room and breakfast. It is a lovely location and a nice room. I arrive too early at the Barns so continue walking into Retford and stumble across an Asda where I can buy another picnic tea—very enjoyable, and I get nice discount buying items that are about to go out of date.

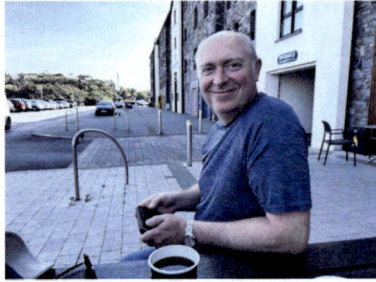

Andrew: It was nice to be back into a routine of regular calls through the day. And I'd found some fun from realising if I called him in the rain, it was awkward for him to find his phone through the raingear. He'd also need to hold the phone up at his ear as he'd not bothered charging his headphones, so hands would get wet. Even more comical (clearly only for me) was calling his other phone if he didn't answer the first one in time. Yes, the juvenile humour would reverberate at times purely to keep David in tiptop mental health whilst enduring his journeying of course 😊

News Headlines Context, 6 October 2020

In news headlines, Eddie Van Halen dead: Legendary guitarist dies after battle with throat cancer aged 65. In America, according to a Reuters/Ipsos poll, the majority of Americans think Mr Trump could have avoided infection if he had taken the virus more seriously. The national opinion poll did not show outpouring support for the President beyond Mr Trump's core group of followers, some of whom gathered outside Walter Reed National Military Medical Centre, where he had been hospitalised. Among those who are expected to cast their vote on November 3, the poll found that 51% were backing his Democratic rival, Joe Biden, while 41% said they were voting for Mr Trump.

"MPs tonight voted 287 to 17, in favour of keeping the regulation ahead of a vote on the 10:00 p.m. curfew on hospitality venues next week. Of those 17, 12 Tory MPs voted against the Government in combination with five DUP MPs. The rules are already in force although MPs were given powers to vote on coronavirus restrictions put forward by the Government in the future. The UK has purchased one million new DIY coronavirus testing kits that can produce results in 20 minutes. The DIY kits will be crucial for helping scientists and politicians understand how far the virus has spread through British society. The kit uses a pin-prick blood sample that can collect data on the numbers of people who have coronavirus. Currently, most coronavirus tests require a swab taken from the back of the nasal cavity or the throat."

Tracking new cases 17,071; deaths 70

(source: coronavirus.data.gov.uk)

The new DIY testing kit seems a step forward—I would prefer a pinprick blood sample rather than the swab approach. The curfew on hospitality should not really affect me as I am in bed by that time—it is the closure of locations that may do.

Church—Laxton.

Waterproofs time.

Bothamsall defibrillator.

No cars—Elkesley.

River Poulter.

Picnic tea. (Maybe too much but it was discounted!)

Six Days Before Arriving at Milestone Two

Day 24. Wednesday 7 October (Morton to Doncaster)

I have a lovely and calorie-dense, full English breakfast, to set me on my way and the sunshine has returned. I have not quite tuned myself fully into technology and how best to use it and so I still have wires all over the place. I have a phone in each pocket (one for calls/Strava and one for navigation) and then I have a portable charger in my bum-bag (so I suppose that is me embracing technology) and then I charge each phone as and when needed during the day. With the navigation phone, the battery lasts around an hour max, so it usually ends up on a charge for most of the day.

I see some very impressive hedges today in Babworth near Retford; perfectly straight and aligned and for quite a long stretch of road too. Whoever trims those hedges has an eye for detail and some seriously strong biceps. I know from experience as a teenager cutting hedges at the family home in Malvern how tiring this can be. Dad used to have a petrol hedge trimmer, and it was quite large as I recall as the hedges were big and overhead height.

They were significantly taller than my height—not just Tim's—so when cutting the hedge tops it felt like lifting a medicine ball over your head and swinging back and forth. However, logically having raised it frequently above head height (and always very safely) I should have much bigger biceps than the balls of cotton wool I have today. Matthew and James, through working out at the gym, have much more impressive biceps and any of my victories in play wrestling from me come when I catch them by surprise and then run away.

I come across a Starbucks mid-morning so I can rest and enjoy a latte—very kindly donated by the store manager at Worksop, and it is a good job that the KFC next door is not open as that would have been highly tempting. I am not sure how I got into my coffee timing craving, but I love a latte in that late morning period between 11.00 to 11.30. I'm not sure why.

I do not feel like one with breakfast, or in the afternoon, but my tongue goes dry, and I feel a real craving as I approach the late morning time slot. A lovely and much healthier alternative to the KFC is my tasty cherry and banoffee pie NAKD bar kindly donated by NAKD. The banoffee pie bar is scrumptious.

The sky clouds over as I reach the outskirts of Doncaster, and it is nice to see a Jewson delivery truck passing by (I am still very loyal to the brands that I have worked for). I have time for a quick lunch and tuck into a nice ploughman's lunch in The Styrrup pub that is kindly donated by the pub landlord. I am staying tonight with friends Alison and Jeff; Anne drives up to visit and brings my large (new) rucksack and extra stuff. It is nice to stay with people for a change and sit on a sofa to watch TV and chat. Another 18 miles on the mileometer tracker walking from Retford to Doncaster.

News Headlines Context, 7 October 2020

In news headlines, Brexit breakthrough: Britain on verge of the trade deal as EU about to make a huge compromise. Hopes of a Brexit deal are growing with Boris Johnson's officials on the verge of another breakthrough in the trade and security talks with Brussels. Dinosaur discovery: Palaeontologists unearth carnivores with crocodile-like senses. Dinosaur experts have announced how an ancient reptile boasted sensory capabilities extraordinarily similar to a modern-day crocodile.

Palaeontologists made the discovery after analysing the fossilised skin of a 155-million-year-old carnivorous dinosaur The juvenile Juravenator dinosaur dates from the Jurassic period and was unearthed in Germany.

Coronavirus Daily Context, 7 October 2020

"There is gloomy data that shows 161 cases per million people in the UK yesterday—20% more than the 134 cases per million reported in the US in the same 24-hour period. It is the first time Britain has recorded more infections per capita than the US since the pandemic began to sweep across the country. Health Secretary Matt Hancock is set to unveil a new three-tier local-level 'COVID alert' system for local areas. It is believed the new system is being brought in to

streamline coronavirus guidelines and give more powers to authorities to slam cities with draconian lockdown measures. It comes as the UK's coronavirus cases have started rising at levels higher than the initial outbreak, along with the controversy over missing cases due to errors with spreadsheets."

Tracking new cases 18,326; deaths 101

(source: coronavirus.data.gov.uk)

One of those records that you do not want to shout about! The rate of acceleration of infections and deaths is quite frightening. If I were walking with a group of fellow walkers, then I would seriously contemplate stopping—not for my own sake as I consider myself able to fight it (rightly or wrongly) but for the risk of contributing the transmission to others.

There may be an impact for me staying with friends/family as planned, but currently, this has not been banned, and I can still meet people outdoors.

Sun peeking through.

Perfect hedges—Babworth.

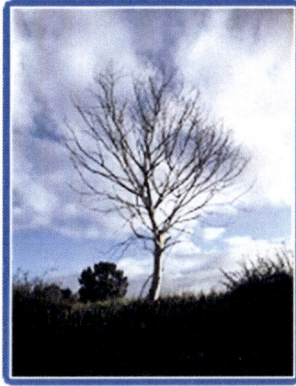

The contrast of tree against the sky.

Jewson delivery!

Five Days Before Arriving
at Milestone Two

Day 25. Thursday 8 October (Doncaster to Deighton with Lift Part Way to Avoid Walking on A1)

I start again with another great breakfast cooked by Alison. Unfortunately, no sunshine today so the waterproofs are back on. I walk through Doncaster town centre but probably do not see it at its best.

There is a significant difference when I think about the different town and city centres that I have visited so far. Some come across as vibrant and engaging—St Albans, for example, while others seem quite depressing, bleak almost, with a lot of closed premises—such as Doncaster. Towns and cities have the challenge to identify what their vision is and what they want to stand for. For sure, the rapid growth in online shopping has created a real challenge, but it is another example of rapid growth from an online challenger business model competing with a traditional, conventional business.

There are lots of examples in the business world, the loss of the Kodak brand to digital cameras, the demise of Blockbuster videos and DVD to Netflix, the closure of multiple clothes and department stores to online brands, which offer ease and convenience. I know there has been a lot of work done by various people to study how we can regenerate our high streets. The Mary Portas vision from a few years ago focused on putting back the high street at the heart of every community, bringing people together.

Mary Portas said in 2011:

"I don't want to live in a Britain that doesn't care about the community. And I believe that our high streets are a really important part of pulling people together in a way that a supermarket or shopping mall, however convenient, however entertaining and however slick, just never can.

Our high streets can be lively, dynamic, exciting and social places that give a sense of belonging and trust to a community. Something which, as the recent riots clearly demonstrated, has been eroded and in some instances eradicated.

I fundamentally believe that once we invest in and create social capital in the heart of our communities, the economic capital will follow.

The recommendations aim to:

1. *Get town centres running like businesses.*
2. *Get the basics right to allow businesses to flourish.*
3. *Level the playing field.*
4. *Define landlords' roles and responsibilities.*
5. *Give communities a greater say."*

I think there is some truth here but also there needs to be recognition that the world—and people's needs—are quite different today than they were even just a few years ago. People are fundamentally gregarious and want to congregate so for me, the creation of a beating heart and a community is the key to regenerating the high street. I am not convinced though that people want to go out physically to shop—some segments of the market do for sure, but the rapid growth of on-online shopping, which has only accelerated in COVID times, will continue; it is easy and convenient, and the time saved can be used to have fun. Anne and the boys do much of their shopping online.

I think that the essence of the high street should be to create experiences where people, families, friends can form long-lasting memories. So dining, pubs, food and drink tastings, singing, dancing, themed nights celebrating different cultural food and drinks nights could all become the beating heart of the modern town/city centre. Perhaps a Brazilian beach night one week and a Greek Taverna night the following week. This would be easier in summer rather than winter but even in the latter, several marquees with outdoor heaters can create a conducive environment.

Activities could also be a core element of the regeneration—maybe a ten-pin bowling competition or a boules tournament with food and drinks. Outdoor pantos at Christmas time, outdoor theatre, fairground, or circus events. If these are planned, publicised, and marketed (I am happy to help here) then I am sure this can bring in the crowds and people will be able to socialise and share memories. Of course, this will have to be post-COVID.

If you look at coffee shops as an example, they have reinvented themselves and indeed thrived whilst home consumption of coffee has also increased. People like to meet for a coffee and a chat; sit on a nice sofa and spend over £3 on a cup that would cost them 50p at home. Why? It is the overall experience. I do it myself—I enjoy people watching, meeting a friend for coffee and a catch-up and feel that I am saving money by collecting my tokens whereas I am spending £2.50 more per coffee than if I sat at home and drank it. Perhaps Boris may give me a call to pull a task force together when I return.

Back to the walk. I do see a strange sight when I come across the structural frame of a house with lots of birds sitting on the structure—it looks like a giant aviary or large birdhouse. It reminds me of the Hitchcock film *The Birds*, and I must add that to my playlist when I return home. The photo does not really do it justice. I am lucky enough to come across a coffee shop today in Askern although not one of my usual haunts (Starbucks, Costa or independent coffee shops)—today I see a table and two chairs outside a florist, and they fortunately serve coffee.

So, I have a latte with toasted teacake, which are donated by the owner—the generosity and kindness of people is truly overwhelming. I see a café in my name—perhaps this is a sign as to what my future career next steps should be. Following my comments yesterday on the impressive hedges in the Doncaster region I also come across the potential architect of this (at least I am assuming this is the hedge trimmer guy as it's too much of a coincidence). He is certainly very thorough although perhaps his reach does not extend to the height of the hedges from yesterday.

I walk the planned 17 miles and then meet Anne, who drives us the last few miles after I have reached my target for the day, to the White Swan at Deighton, enabling me to avoid walking on the A1. Many thanks for the donation of a room and breakfast at a time when the business is struggling to keep going due to the coronavirus impact and consequent lack of customers.

News Headlines Context, 8 October 2020

In news headlines, EU civil war: Germany under attack with a bid to end a bitter row over bloc's coronavirus fund. The European Union is embroiled in a bitter row over its next seven-year budget with Germany under attack for its attempt to end the deadlock. The bloc's three institutions—the Council,

Commission and Parliament—are locked in talks to finalise the planned €1.8trillion recovery fund and budget package before the end of the year. Germany, which holds the EU's rotating presidency, has proposed the possibility of billions of euros extra spending in a bid to break the deadlock with the EU Parliament over ensuring a clear link between funding and the rule of law. HMRC warning: SEISS 'fraud' could soar to over £250million—impact on Britons. SEISS, otherwise known as the Self-Employment Income Support Scheme, has provided support to many people throughout the COVID-19 pandemic. However, many claims could be incorrectly or fraudulently conducted.

Coronavirus Daily Context, 8 October 2020

The Prime Minister is expected to divide the country into three tiers depending on the risk and the rate of infections. Areas such as Liverpool, Manchester and Newcastle have seen cases soar over recent weeks. Pubs and bars across the country all currently have a 10:00 p.m. curfew but harsher measures could soon be imposed. Summary of the rules:

England-wide rules include:

No gatherings of more than six people.

A 10:00 p.m. curfew for pubs, restaurants and bars hospitality restrictions to table service only work from home advised wherever possible.

Compulsory face masks for people in shops or hospitality settings Fines for not wearing masks increased to £200 for first offences Specific local areas people have to abide by the following rules: No mixing with other households in homes or garden.

No mixing with other households in indoor public venues such as pubs No mixing with other households outdoors.

No walk-ins for pubs and restaurants.

No visits to care homes unless in exceptional circumstances Children of separated parents may move between households.

Funerals limited to no more than 30 attendants.

"Weddings limited to no more than 15 guests."

Tracking new cases 18,246; deaths 92

(Source: coronavirus.data.gov.uk)

I wonder what the logic is to allow double the number of attendees to attend a funeral, compared with only 15 guests allowed to celebrate the supposedly 'happier' occasion of a wedding? One small consolation in the 'not do' list is that they are not directly affecting my plan yet. All my hotel, pub and bed and breakfast locations are planned versus walk-in. I do not have any work from home restrictions as I am not working, and I am not at home. The worry for me continues to be the pace of the new restrictions coming in and where/when they will impact me.

There is a lot of talk around challenges in the North of England, which is where I am heading. It feels a little like one of those tornado or hurricane films where you see the scientists rushing towards the eye of the tornado to capture data. It is exhilarating, intoxicating but if you get caught in the middle then you will not be around for very long to share your learning. It feels that I am headed right towards the centre of the COVID explosion.

Grumpy Dave's café.

Large Aviary—Toll Bar.

112

First coffee from a florist! Askern

Balne

The impressive hedge trimmer?

Lovely church—Whitley

Whitley Green field and dramatic sky—Kellington.

Four Days Before Arriving at Milestone Two

Day 26. Friday 9 October: Deighton to Easingwold (with Lift for Part Way)

Anne and I have a nice chat with the owner that results in a change of plan for my walk today. Instead of walking on the A19 itself, he drives me 5 miles to be able to walk the Trans Pennine way and into York. I get potential inspiration for a future walk, although the distance could perhaps be a step too far for me— Uranus is 1,443,300,000 km away, and Jupiter is probably more realistic at only 648,860,000 km. Fantastic—no cars or lorries and a very peaceful walk via the York racecourse.

It is lovely to walk across the racecourse and picture the horses pounding across the course at speed with hooves flying. This proves to be one of my most enjoyable days walking so far. York is one of my favourite cities—I have spent a lot of time here with Matthew (coordinating pub and dinner visits when dropping him or collecting him from university); I had a 'boys' weekend' here with my brother and sons also and have met up with my ex-Jewson colleagues for dinner several times.

As I mentioned earlier it is important to have personal time with key people in your life. 'Boys weekends' are a good example of this although the definition of who attends has certainly evolved, and it is high on my agenda to organise multiple and frequent events (pre-COVID). The first ones started when the children were young, and it was basically a chance for my Dad, me, and my brothers to get away for one or two nights a year. We would alternate the organisation and visited hotels in Kent, Stratford, Banbury, and Chester to name but a few.

They are not 'heavy sessions' but as neither Tim nor Andrew play golf, they tend to revolve around watching a big football or rugby match, playing cards, drinking beer, gin, and wine, and having a laugh. We would often take advantage of the local cinema to catch up with the latest blockbusters—we all enjoy ice cream, and the challenge would be to see who had not spilt it down their tops by the time we leave the cinema. It is usually Andrew or me, and often both, who emerge with damp patches on our shirts where we have smudged the mint choc chip with bits of tissue.

One particular highlight for me was when we visited Banbury, and there were no stand-out films available that one of us had not seen. So, we ended up plumping for the matinee at 11:00 am on Saturday. I think the film was something like *The Lion, the Witch and the Wardrobe*, and there were hundreds of children under the age of about 8—most with their parents—and then three six-foot-tall Fentons (plus Tim) sitting together in the centre of a middle row looking very conspicuous and probably a bit suspicious. Mind you we were sitting with one of our parents also!

Stratford has been a popular location for us as we have visited two or three times for our boys' weekend. One such occasion was a stag boys' weekend prior to Andrew and Hilary getting married; Dad bought Andrew an 'inconspicuous' green and red jester hat, and he had to wear it for the rest of the weekend in public. Following the eventful weekend in Chester (hereafter known as 'Chestergate') which was our final 'oldies boys' weekend' in 2018, the opportunities for the four of us to meet seem over as Dad has now retired and Andrew lives in Dublin. I must take responsibility for Chester as I booked it.

The B&B was quite small with single beds and rafters within inches of the head of the beds resulting in a few bangs, bumps and bruises. I think this was a key factor in Dad formally retiring from the 'oldies boys' weekends. But I am not defeated and end up having separate boys' weekends with Andrew and/or Tim and my boys as well. I will always make the time.

Tim and I had a great one in 2019 in Birmingham. It was in November and the Christmas market was a thriving hub of activity with an array of beers, liquors and German sausage with sauerkraut combinations assaulting our senses. We saw a couple of good films and had some nice meals. Tim had booked us into the Premier Inn near the Bullring. Well, we thought it was 'the' hotel, however, on Saturday night as we returned to the hotel, the key card would not open our room number. We had a room card each so we both tried but the door would not budge.

We double-checked the room number in case we were a floor above or below where we should be. Probably the key cards had been next to one of our mobile phones. We went back to reception to ask for new keys and discovered they had no record of our booking. It materialised that the keys did work, and the bedroom door worked—it is just that they were in a different hotel to the one we were standing in! We had somehow walked to a similar-looking Premier Inn hotel also near the Bullring—so now all we had to do was find the right bedroom door in the right hotel. Amusing in hindsight but not at the time.

I also love going away with Matthew and James. We tend to do an activity such as walking or cycling and play board games also, so we have been up Snowdon, walked in the Lake District, spent time in York and visited Weymouth. Weymouth was a great break as we managed to get a bedroom for the three of us, and it was overlooking the seafront. I also knew that Andrew was going to do a surprise visit one evening, and I manipulated the seating in the pub so that when he walked in, they did not see his face until he was at the table.

Then we tucked into our pints of lager and packets of pork scratchings. I am not sure what the secret recipe of these weekends is, but I will be disappointed when they stop. I do not envisage that I will ever retire from these weekends. We have obviously not been able to do one in 2020 and I really miss them. I think it is a combination of a nice location, camaraderie and Christmas cracker jokes combined with cinema, alcohol, sport and games that contribute to creating magical memories.

York is a lovely city with some fantastic pubs and a thriving, bustling culture. So, it feels very strange to pass through and walk past the pubs I know, rather than walk into them. I meet Anne in Easingwold, which is slightly further north out of the city—I really like the town/village (it's picturesque but bigger than I thought it would be). Anne and I have a late lunch at Fika café which kindly donates lunch when they hear our story.

I have a few miles still to achieve my target, so I walk around the Easingwold area to achieve the planned 15 miles and then ease into my established post-walk routine of stretch, shower (sometimes combining the two together), Epsom salts, ice the feet and follow up with a couple of pints. I have found the routine of managing my feet seems to be paying dividends. The process of icing the feet where possible and elevating them above my head level seems to be paying dividends. Staying at the George in Easingwold they kindly discount the rate for bed and breakfast, and we have a lovely meal in the restaurant, so no walking is required. It is great to have some company.

News Headlines Context, 9 October 2020

In news headlines, Joe Biden is on the brink as Donald Trump landslide on cards after 'voting intentions unmasked'. Joe Biden could suffer the same fate as Hilary Clinton by seeing a big lead turn into defeat as Donald Trump earns encouragement from a surprising poll. While the former Vice President's position looks increasingly commanding, a Fox News poll could offer encouragement for President Trump—meaning his route to a dream election landslide could still be open.

A growing number of Americans think their neighbours support Mr Trump over Mr Biden in the upcoming election, according to the survey. It found that 49% thought their neighbours were supporting Mr Trump for president. By comparison, 38% of respondents said they thought their neighbours were backing the Biden campaign.

Coronavirus Daily Context, 9 October 2020

In news headlines, Britain is back where it was in March as hospitals fill up with COVID-19 patients, the deputy chief medical officer for England has warned. Jonathan Van-Tam said intensive care units in the northwest of England could fill up in less than a month. Daily hospitalisations are currently around the same level as they were in the days leading up to 23 March, when the UK first went into full lockdown. As further lockdown restrictions appear likely, this week the Chancellor announced the Government's Job Support Scheme will be expanded.

"If a business is forced to close, such as in the case of a local lockdown, Mr Sunak stated workers will receive two-thirds of their wages. The scheme will begin on November 1 and will be available for six months, with a review point scheduled for January. Mr Sunak said: 'Throughout this crisis, my priority has always been to protect jobs so today I'm announcing an expansion of our Jobs Support Scheme, specifically to protect those jobs of people who work in businesses who may be asked to close'."

Tracking new cases 15,731; deaths 79
(Source: coronavirus.data.gov.uk)

I am certainly seeing the impact of COVID in the places where I am staying—both in terms of fewer people on the premises and the impact it has on the pub/hotel owners' income. There are no winners as a result of this virus except perhaps PPE and virus vaccine manufacturers.

Matthew: Sometimes when I phoned him, he sounded chipper, sometimes he sounded spent and those were the hardest calls to have, trying to cheer him up and help him get through. It always worried me him being out on his own all the time. I think he was lucky to have all the phone calls from his brothers and parents and they must have helped him a lot.

Leaving the White Swan.

Uranus or Jupiter?

River at Bishopthorpe

York city centre.

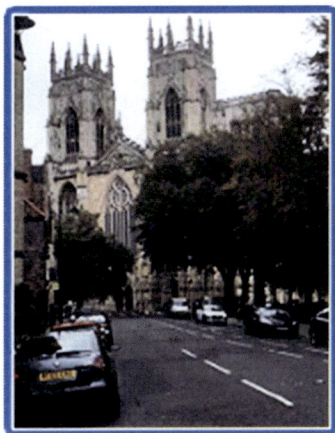

York cathedral.

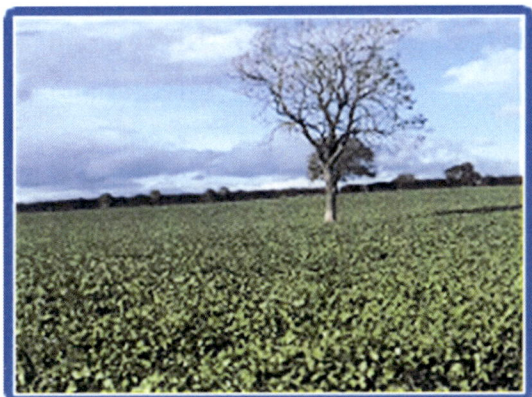

Love the rich colours—Easingwold.

Three Days Before Arriving at Milestone Two

Day 27. Saturday 10 October, Easingwold to Carthorpe

A lovely (healthier) breakfast today of scrambled eggs and salmon to start the day, and I have my longest walk since returning to the trek at 21 miles. Some great scenic views today although I sometimes wonder if I am overdoing the photographic evidence of the beautiful fields we have in this country.

I find it interesting to reflect how this walk reflects the path of life in several ways. For example, I have a plan, but I regularly veer off course, there are good days and bad days (fortunately more of the former than the latter), the subject of 'choice' is particularly relevant. Each day I work out which of the three routes presented by Google Maps I will take (or I could potentially even 'ad lib' and take my own route not those options presented to me—although I do not). The route that I walk, the people that I meet, the photographs that I take are all the results of that choice.

By not taking one of the other two available routes then I have no idea what I have missed—would one of them have created a more memorable experience than the walk I selected? I will never know. The choice is defined as 'an act or the possibility of choosing' (*Cambridge Dictionary*), and in life, we are making choices and decisions each day. The career that I have had in sales and marketing is the result of my choice to leave the civil service after nine months as a management trainee and join Black and Decker as a graduate sales executive.

Combined with the company's decision whether to choose me or an alternative candidate for the job. If I had not made that choice then maybe I would have progressed in the civil service to become senior civil servant, a 'Sir Humphrey' as per the Yes Minister series (which is one of the reasons that I think I applied there in the first place). The impact and implications of making a choice, right or wrong, good, or bad, lucky, or unlucky is huge and you do not always appreciate that at the time. I have set my milestone targets and then plan the detail of the routes between the milestones. Similarly, most people have goals for themselves whether personal, and or professional, and then make decisions that either help or hinder them to achieve their goals.

Some of the scenes from today are a blend or contrast of rich colours. The shots are so vivid, blending the shades of grey/white/blue in the sky with the pastel green colours of the trees and fields. The photograph in Brafferton looks like a Monet watercolour painting with the light colours seemingly brushed onto the canvas creating the woodland scene. I get drenched a couple of times today, but the waterproofs soon dry out and my walking shoes do their job in protecting my feet.

My walk today is again on the quieter roads so very few vehicles about—long may this continue. Tomorrow is a rest day—well deserved even if I do say so myself. I like the blend of nature and man-made materials with the photo of the post-box morphed into the hedge—the red and green combination seems to work with each highlighting the other nicely. I meet with Anne for a coffee and then continue my journey to Paul's house (Anne's brother) who kindly puts me up for a few nights as I tackle the Yorkshire leg of the walk.

I enjoy the contrasting perspective in the late afternoon of the cloudy sky, wet road, and emerging sun—providing an array of colours and shapes, and it is unlikely I would even have noticed such views had I been driving. I arrive at Paul and Ros's in the late afternoon, and I enjoy having some time getting to know my nephews better and being able to watch TV—they have the Disney channel, so I enjoy a couple of episodes of the Mandalorian. I also become a convert to Black Sheep beer as I help Paul to free up some space in his fridge!

News Headlines Context, 10 October 2020

In news headlines, Egypt breakthrough: Great Pyramid tipped for a major discovery in new 'hidden chamber' scan.

Egypt's Great Pyramid of Giza could be at the centre of a major breakthrough as experts are poised to confirm if there is a mysterious 'internal chamber'. The 4,500-year-old pyramid is the oldest and largest of the three ancient monuments in the Giza Plateau and is believed to have been constructed for Pharaoh Khufu over a 20-year period. The ScanPyramids project was launched to provide several non-invasive and non-destructive techniques, which may help provide a better understanding of its structure and the construction processes and techniques.

"After two years of work, French experts announced the discovery of the 'Big Void', a 30-metre previously unknown cavity located above the Grand Gallery. The royal mystery unravelled as a puzzle of Richard III's burial site solved. Royal family history was changed forever when King Richard III's remains were found in a Leicester car park in 2012—and the geneticist and archaeologist who was on site explained the astounding circumstances surrounding the discovery. Archaeologist and geneticist Dr Turi King, who helped to identify Richard's remains noted that Richard had assembled his troops in Leicester before he went to battle—he wanted to deter Henry Tudor's forces before he got to London. She explained: 'It's the nearest big city, it's the last place Richard was really seen alive, and if you want people to know, 'yep, this is Richard III and he's actually died', you would want to bring him back to a city'."

Coronavirus Daily Context, 10 October 2020

"In news headlines, the UK's hospital death toll has soared by 81, with the Prime Minister due to set out tougher restrictions for millions of Britons from next week. England has recorded 60 more deaths in hospitals, Wales 21, and Scotland a further six. Northern Ireland has reported no more fatalities. This has increased from last Saturday when there were 51 deaths recorded in the UK's hospitals and is the highest rise since late June. The Prime Minister is set to announce more localised restrictions on Monday, as pubs and restaurants across northern England are widely expected to be told to shut to limit the spread of coronavirus. Coronavirus lockdown warning: all obese people in their 50s could be forced to shield."

Tracking new cases 12,515; deaths 103
(Source: coronavirus.data.gov.uk)

I am worried about the rumours of closed pubs and restaurants in the north of England—unfortunately, I have no room in my backpack for a tent unless it is one that can wrap itself into a small hand-sized ball without the need for struts and poles. Now maybe that is an innovative idea for a new business upon my return. I turn over the options in my mind should the pandemic scupper my accommodation.

I could aim for a part of England where there are no restrictions and do the walk there. Maybe around my home or potentially near my parents. However, it would cost me the essence of the walk—'Miles, Milestones and Memories'—if I must do that then I could still achieve the miles target but not the milestones or memories.

Lovely silhouette—Raskelf.

Looks like a watercolour painting—Brafferton.

Nature & man-made in sync.

Me with 'Support team'.

Beautiful shades of green.

Topcliffe

Saturday night with Paul.

Day 28. Sunday 11 October—Rest Day! One Day Before Arriving at Milestone Two

Day 29. Monday 12 October, Carthorpe to Healey back to Carthorpe

Again, I decided that rather than walking up the A1 I will walk the miles around Carthorpe and then stay another evening at Paul's house. I notice an interesting use of space in the wall of one of Paul's neighbours—a cubbyhole effectively being used as a storage for book exchange—a great idea. Today I am in the middle of nowhere with a multitude of pheasants and cows.

An amusing sight hits me walking through the village of Well near Bedale where the homeowner parks his tractor outside the front door on the pavement rather than the traditional car. I walk past the Black Sheep beer visitor centre and factory—I try to call in and pay a visit as I really enjoyed the samples, I shared with Paul on Saturday evening, but unfortunately, it is closed on a Monday and Tuesday. I am disappointed as I am about to proffer my services as either a sample taster or salesperson.

There is an interesting story as the backdrop to Black Sheep, which Paul shared with me on Saturday night, and which is captured on their website:

In 1992, Paul Theakston took a daring leap into the unknown. As a fifth-generation brewer of his family company, he chose to leave T&R Theakstons following its sale to a national brewery. Instead, he chose to champion independent brewing in Yorkshire and built his own brewery from reclaimed equipment in the very same town, Masham.

Paul is the Black Sheep.

Set in an old malting overlooking the town, the brewery was built using a brewing kit sourced from old breweries plus a lot of heart and soul. The very same equipment is still used to this day, brewing some of your favourite Black Sheep beers that are available across the nation.

Our award-winning range of beers is an eclectic mix of classic and modern styles as we continue to champion innovation whilst staying true to our traditional roots.

We brew beer in cask, keg, bottle, can and mini-keg and constantly strive to create beers that excite our drinkers. In what is today a very different brewing industry from what it once was, we fully embrace what is an exciting, dynamic and diverse world and will continue to do what we love. Brew great beer.

Today, Black Sheep continues to champion its independence and remains with Paul Theakston's family as Rob—Paul's eldest son—runs the brewery as Managing Director whilst Jo—Paul's second eldest son—holds the role of Sales & Marketing Director. In 2018, Paul stepped down from the board to take up his ambassadorial role as the founder of Black Sheep and remains a vital part of the company.

(Source: www.blacksheepbrewery.com/our-story/the-story/)

It tastes great!

The other good thing about walking effectively in a circle and returning to Carthorpe is that I do not need to take the big 85-litre rucksack on my back. I walk over 20 miles to achieve my target and return to a home-cooked meal in the evening and more episodes of the Mandalorian.

News Headlines Context, 12 October 2020

In news headlines, World War III fears: Japan vows to boost missile defence after North Korea military parade. World War 3 fears have been ignited with Japan vowing to boost its missile defences after North Korea showcased their military might during a parade. The Arctic Ocean is dying' Scientist's dire warning after biggest North Pole expedition yet. The Arctic Ocean is dying and climate change is to blame, scientists have announced after concluding the world's biggest expedition to the North Pole.

Coronavirus Daily Context, 12 October 2020

Chris Whitty has urged the British public to work together to lower coronavirus cases after Boris Johnson announced a three-tier system for the UK. The chief medical officer explained that while the measures put in place will help slow the spread of COVID-19, more needs to be done by local authorities. He noted that the tiers have scope for local leaders to work with the directors of public health and impose measures suited to the area.

"Coronavirus could be prevalent across the UK until 2022 as government's are preparing contingency plans to deal with its spread. Track and trace staff are being hired on 18-month contracts over fears that Coronavirus could be rolling on for months on end. The contracts, revealed in online job adverts, suggest that health chiefs are preparing for the pandemic to continue at least into 2022."

Tracking new cases 19,447; deaths 112
(source: coronavirus.data.gov.uk).

It seems sensible to me to plan on the basis that the consequences of the virus could continue into 2022 until there is a clear solution and timetable on the vaccine(s). I am pleased that Yorkshire is not (yet) classified in the third tier of restrictions, so it is still OK for me to stay with Paul and his family.

Neighbourly library.

Local steak!

Kerbside parking.

Well River Ure.

A climbing ladder/tree!

Black Sheep brewery.

Lift to Bishop Auckland to Milestone Two

Day 30. Tuesday 13 October

It is back to reality today as I must prepare my own breakfast (and rightly so in a house with the fun, also known as mayhem, of getting kids ready for school) so porridge and jam on toast set me off nicely. I avoid the A1 again thanks to getting a lift from Ros (combined with a school drop off) to Bishop Auckland. From there I can complete the 12 miles I plan to walk today.

A very wet day. It is strange to walk through Spennymoor town centre as I have never been through the town itself before. I would come to this area frequently when working for Black & Decker as we had, at the time, a power tool manufacturing plant in the area. Spennymoor town is much larger than I had thought but still only has one coffee shop with about three 'socially distant' tables (all occupied despite me looking forlorn, gaunt, thirsty, and haggard staring through the shop window hoping for some sympathy and somebody to exit). I was desperate for a coffee—it was that late morning slot when I need to have a caffeine boost—and being able to see it through the café window, I could also smell and taste it. I would rather it had been shut so that my expectations could not be raised.

Nevertheless, I top up my jelly baby dosage and walk on through to my destination without taking a break. I have also agreed with Paul, that as I will be doubling back on myself at a later date, then I will stay with them again on Friday and treat them all to a Chinese takeaway as a thank you for their hospitality. It also means that I can get away with the day rucksack and more clothes washing by hand and so can leave the large rucksack at Paul's. I come across an amusing sign in Brandon, the 'Honest Lawyer Hotel' which is either an oxymoron or perhaps aiming at a very niche target market.

In 1985, I began three of the best years of my life—the university years. Always a challenging time to know what you want to do and where you want to go. I had no idea what I wanted to do for a job. I did know that I wanted to build my independence and enjoyed Economics. I tried for Cambridge but flunked the interview. My grades were anticipated to be good—and were with 3 A's—but not enough. Lancaster was my fallback university if I had missed out on my first choice.

Here I am walking into the city where I attended university—my second milestone—but with no idea where I am or which part of the city I will enter. It turns out that I arrive at the back end of the city near the viaduct, which as a student was never one of our chosen hanging out spots. I have time for a nice burger lunch and am incredibly grateful to the waitress who kindly donates her tips to me.

It is **Durham**!

Milestone two reached! Part of me can, unfortunately, hear Andrew singing the dulcet tones of Roger Whittaker singing "I'm going to leave old Durham town," but I successfully block that out.

I owe many thanks to the Victorian Town House which donates bed and breakfast to me even though the owners are starting to wind down their business now. I stay the following night as well (paid this time) so that I can leave my gear and my clothes drying in one place. I enjoy a quick walk around the town and have a couple of pints in the Swan and Three Cygnets—for old times' sake combined with the fact it is only £3 a pint. Oh, the good old days! On the other hand, several pubs are shut due to COVID (Dun Cow for example) which is a shame. I have a lovely Indian meal at a restaurant I have not visited before—there are only 2 customers in while I eat, and it is clearly not related to the quality of the food, which is lovely.

I had 3 fantastic years at St Hild and Bede College from 1985 to 1988—that's why it was such an easy choice for milestone two—and I am so much looking forward to seeing what remains. I have scheduled Wednesday as a 'rest day' although that basically means walking around Durham and the sights.

> Andrew: I had been looking forward to David reaching Goal 2; Durham. I'd visited him a few times whilst he was there at university. It's a long way up North for sure. I'd also enjoyed practicing singing Roger Whittaker's Durham Town song. I delivered this in full gusto when he picked up my first call of the day. I am sure that it was appreciated!

News Headlines Context, 13 October 2020

In news headlines, Leonardo da Vinci unmasked: Hidden dots expose secret alterations to Mona Lisa. Leonardo Da Vinci made a series of dots and marks on the Mona Lisa that allowed him to make secret alterations to the world-renowned painting, a scientist sensationally revealed. Scientist Pascal Cotte, who digitised the painting and spent a decade studying it, believes his findings answer some of those questions. Using a high-definition camera and a specialist technique, he discovered hidden marks that indicate changes da Vinci made to the world-famous artwork. His technique, which detected how light interacts with the paint, allowed him to view 'different layers' of the piece and find previously hidden features.

Coronavirus Daily Context, 13 October 2020

WHO says COVID herd immunity 'unethical' but also rejects lockdown... so what does it want? Coronavirus has infected more than 37 million people and killed more than a million others around the world, but seven months after the global pandemic began, the WHO is no closer to outlining a clear strategy to tackle COVID-19. When do new COVID rules start? The new three-tier system will come into force from 12:01 a.m. on Wednesday, 14 October. Most areas currently under a local lockdown or additional restrictions will be placed under Tier 2 restrictions from this date.

"A few other areas, such as Nottinghamshire, are being upgraded to Tier 2 restrictions as well. The Liverpool City region will be the only part of the country to face Tier 3 restrictions from Wednesday. Under the highest tier, people living in the region will not be able to socialise with other people from outside their households in indoor settings. Pubs and bars will also have to close temporarily unless they can operate as a restaurant. Other venues will also be closing across Liverpool City, including gyms, casinos and betting shops."

Tracking new cases 18,904; deaths 109

(Source: coronavirus.data.gov.uk).

So Liverpool is in the toughest tier three category—I very nearly included Liverpool in my journey as I worked there for several months as a management trainee in the Department of Employment in the late 1980s—good job it didn't quite make my top milestones list!

DIY breakfast to start the day.

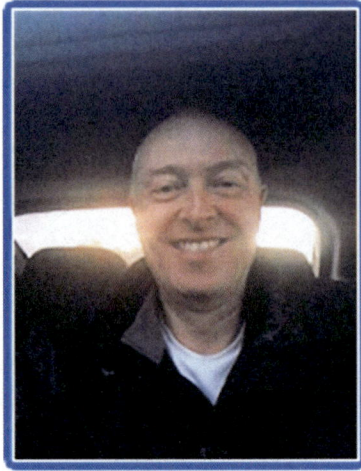

Lift to the start of walk.

Raining in Bishop Auckland.

Bishop Auckland cemetery

Croxdale Hall.

Great sign—Brandon.

Durham

Arrival at Victorian Townhouse—very wet.

Day 31. Wednesday 14 October, Rest Day

Today is a combination of a rest day and a day of reminiscing (as well as somehow walking 8 miles)—and an opportunity to meet with Stephanie Maurel the alumni officer for the college along with Simon Forrest the current Principal of the college. I spend the morning in the city visiting the obvious attractions of the castle and cathedral. From my recollections of the late '80s the heart of the city remains pretty much the same despite the obvious shop closures that have impacted most town or city centres, the road building and infrastructure change around the city are significant though.

I enjoy a latte in an Italian coffee shop near the bridge—my favoured coffee shop previously had a big window frontage so you could drink coffee and observe life passing by, but the usage is different now, and it is not open in the morning. Certainly, 'Pawsome' a café for cats (see photo) did not exist in my day—I did not go in but wonder if they get a loyalty card offering a free sardine with the consumption of ten saucer lattes.

In the afternoon, I walk around the grounds of St Hild and St Bede college—again not much has changed. I am not allowed inside unfortunately and many of the students are self-isolating in their dorms. It is a bit like a ghost town with so many students from so many colleges locked away across the whole city for a 2-week period. It feels in part that I am walking through an apocalyptic film set.

It is lovely to meet with Simon and Stephanie who have been at the college for less than a couple of years. They are pleased I have visited and so am I—I even get a mention in the alumni magazine. It strikes me how different it is for students today in the COVID period and how lucky I was not to have this particular challenge to combat. I research further on the origins of the college as the only thing that I can recall when applying was ensuring that it was a mixed college.

Originally St Hild and Bede were two separate teaching training colleges—the Durham Diocesan Training School for the Education of Schoolmasters (which is a nice punchy title!) and later became Bede College; and the Durham Diocesan Female Training School, which later became Hild College.

The Durham Diocesan Training School was founded in 1839 and moved to its current site five years later where it was open to local children and helped aspiring teachers to gain work experience. It was renamed Bede College in 1866 and by 1919 it had become a fully licensed hall of residence for the university. A new chapel (still extant today) was created in 1939 and is viewed as one of the university's architectural treasures. Bede was greatly affected by World War 1, with a number of students being drafted into the Durham Light Infantry.

Around 600 men were involved in active service with many present at the Battle of the Somme—indeed the college closed from July 1916 to 1918. It is interesting to read the history and kind of spooky to see the role of the Durham Light Infantry because I can remember clearly the similarly named pub I visited with mum and dad on the day that I started university—the DLI on Gilesgate. I even remember having a toasted sandwich (which I could not finish due to my butterflies) and a pint of lager (which I did finish!)

The Durham Diocesan Female Training school opened in 1858 with only six students. I could imagine the fresher week was probably a little dull! The school became a training college in 1870, becoming College of St Hild in July 1896. It became a licensed hall of residence for the university in 1923 and remained open throughout both world wars.

Both Colleges built a strong reputation for their teaching excellence and while they occasionally co-operated each retained its unique identity. In the 1960s, there was increasing pressure to merge; the libraries were amalgamated, and some joint building works began to take place. In 1975, the colleges finally merged and became the College of St Hild and St Bede where it is now the largest of the Durham colleges, supporting over 1200 undergraduate and postgraduate students. It also has the largest site of all the colleges with sixteen acres of land.

It is fantastic to have been part of the history, and I feel emotionally entwined with the College. It will always be special to me. I feel really sorry for the students today—particularly those just starting out over the last twelve months during the pandemic. The challenges faced by the students are significant during COVID and the follow-up Christmas letter that I received from Simon Forrest captures the challenges—and the positives that often emerge! Simon explained the preparation for the students—setting up 'households' in which freshers would live without having to adopt social distancing rules. The reality was though that everybody was affected by the virus, a number were symptomatically ill, some others infected but did not suffer symptoms.

It required a tremendous logistical plan to organise food and post, and clearly, there was a heavy emotional burden for both staff and particularly students being away from home, sometimes for the first time. Students could not mingle with other colleges, events and infamous formal dinners could not be held. It also impacted the non-resident students who could not utilise the college facilities.

It is not just the tangible events or occasions that are impacted through the pandemic but the consequences of the absence of everyday interaction that would otherwise be treated as 'normal'. It is a challenge to build new relationships and for freshers to forge the close bonds that in many cases will last for their whole lives. Simon says in his regular College update:

"Because each of our worlds has been made much smaller by the constraints thrown around us by a coronavirus and the legislative response and impositions, it has been intense and at times difficult for people to live in these conditions and we have been pressed and compressed in social, emotional and relational life. I want to praise our staff and our students who have coped with all this. We have tried to keep safe, to promote the kind and collegial and not be washed away by circumstances."

As with all adversities, however, there are always positives that emerge! Simon refers to a number of remarkable positives: the regular quiz continued to be run online, the students created a new Literary Society and a Music Society. There is a proposal to create a Sailing Club and take a team to France in 2021. Simon closed his letter recognising the fantastic commitment and spirit of the students, and it is heartening to read about the results achieved during times of hardship—when spirit and creativity come to the fore:

Despite the concomitant pressure to introspection produced by the pandemic and regulatory responses to it, your students have looked out. They raised well over £3000 at the current estimation for 'Movember' in support of the promotion of awareness of men's health. They cooked, ran, dressed up, and much more. The student welfare committee, the communities and liberations committee, and the international student committee have been outstandingly committed to looking after our students.

We have collected large donations for local food banks. Hild Bede Dance, Cheerleading, Theatre and the Boat Club have all produced detailed risk assessments and plans to be able to operate as soon as circumstances and the COVID regulations permit. We will, then, when this dreadful pandemic allows is, be ready to flourish fully once more in action and activity and in spirit.

"In many ways, the pandemic and the rules that it had placed on us are antithetical to the purpose and ethos of the college. They have pushed us apart when our ethos is to be and to pull together."

Simon Forrest

Principal of the College of St Hild and St Bede

I had a fantastic time in Durham—for sure one of the most enjoyable periods of my life. As my parents frequently tell me I left home as a shy, quiet lad and became much more confident and outgoing as time went on.

I was lucky to be living in a detached house owned by the college where we formed a tight group early on and stayed together largely over the 3 years. I am so glad Matthew and James also went a similar route attending York and Exeter, respectively. Like me, they formed close relationships and have matured as their confidence has developed.

For me, it is much less about academic development than personal and social development although perhaps the two are related. I was able to try new things such as rowing as part of an eight crew. It sounds more glamorous than it was, although it certainly helped my fitness. I recall having to be up regularly around 5:00 a.m. in the dark and cold in December—and that is not easy for a student when you have been out the night before. When the rowing session had finished, and we climbed out of the boat I would have ice in my hair (yes, I had hair then and no, it was not greying—it was ice) because the splashes created by the oars would drench our hair and clothes, which would then freeze due to the low temperatures.

At the end of the first term when my father came to collect me all the girls in the building chased me out and tried to catch me for a farewell kiss, which Dad loved and replays back to this day, whoever is in earshot when Durham or University gets mentioned. I caught glandular fever and had to miss the start of the second term—there was discussion about starting the year again but having made such strong friendships I wanted to continue with them and not start over. The formal dinners were a real highlight of college life. I am not really into formality—I prefer wearing jeans to a suit, a T-shirt versus a collared shirt (although that is largely so that I do not have to iron them afterwards)—however, the formal dinners were a great experience.

The numbers that could attend were limited for space reasons, so our group would queue for tickets overnight, taking turns to do a shift and sleep in the corridor. The food was great, the music and dancing usually being a highlight and of course plenty of alcohol. Somehow in those days the stamina came from somewhere and you could play hard, work hard and still find time for sport—today if I attended a formal dinner, I would be out of action for a week.

I have an exciting evening scheduled—a couple of cheaper pints followed by a reserved table right in front of the big screen in the pub to watch England vs. Denmark—unfortunately, the anticipation does not match the reality—it is a rubbish game and ends 0-0.

News Headlines Context, 14 October 2020

In news headlines, France is under pressure to drop its hard-line fishing demands amid fears Emmanuel Macron could scupper hopes of a Brexit deal. European capitals have signalled a willingness to broker a compromise to secure future access to Britain's coastal waters. But Paris was said to be holding out to maintain the status quo for French trawlermen after the end of the transition period in December. The row over fisheries remains one of the biggest stumbling blocks in finding a post-Brexit deal in the coming weeks. Ground-breaking puncture-proof tyre invented—and thousands of cyclists have bought a pair. The new tyre, which has undergone 15 years of research and development, is capable of riding over thorns, nails, potholes and broken glass without suffering a puncture.

Coronavirus Daily Context, 14 October 2020

"Scientists have recommended millions of people across northern England be placed into Tier 3 lockdown—the highest alert level for rising coronavirus cases. The BBC has reported that during a meeting of the joint Biosecurity Council this afternoon, 'lots of areas' were recommended for Tier 3, including

most of the North East, North West, large parts of Yorkshire and some of the Midlands. This is just a recommendation at the moment and has not yet been agreed upon. Several meetings are now being arranged to talk to those regions individually about a possible change in lockdown restrictions."

Tracking new cases 19,709; deaths 116

(Source: coronavirus.data.gov.uk).

The impact of the virus is a moving feast. Only yesterday there was clarity as to which areas fitted into which tiers and today it appears there are multiple, ongoing discussions to rethink this classification—it makes planning ahead almost impossible for everybody concerned. It is such a strange feeling that I am almost walking in a bubble. I read the news and see the rapidly escalating number of infections and deaths.

I realise that any day I may have to replan my walk to avoid an area with high infections or worse miss a milestone. Yet, as I walk the route, it's generally peaceful and quiet—particularly on the smaller roads, and it feels like I am walking on a different planet, almost my own little world.

Durham Cathedral.

Me again!

Durham Cathedral interior.

Durham city centre.

Durham Cathedral.

River Wear Durham.

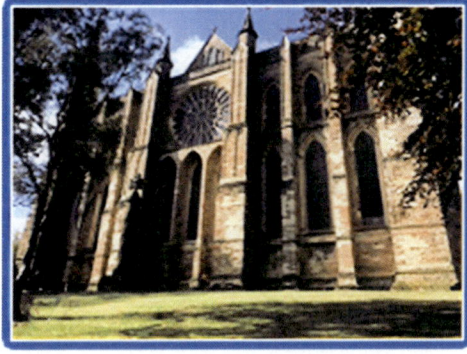

Durham Cathedral.

Café for cats.

St Hild and Bede College.

St Hild & Bede College.

Meeting Simon and Stephanie.

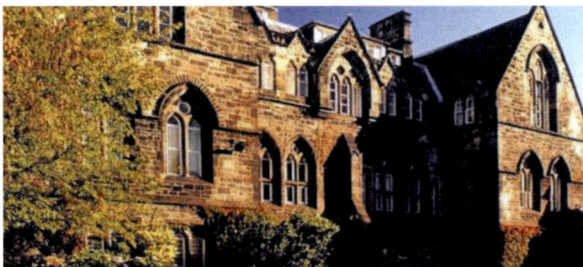

College Photo from St Hild and Bede newsletter.

Seven Days Before Arriving at
Milestone Three

Day 32. Thursday 15 October, Durham to Redworth Hall

I enjoy today's walk. It is a relatively gentle walk of 14 miles and the hotel—Redworth Hall appears on the website like it will be a lovely venue. I come across a garden front wall full of character—it looks like a giant snail—it must have been challenging to design and have required great dexterity and patience to construct the circularity of the wheel effect at the end of the wall. It is uplifting to see the sign for Redworth Hall in the early afternoon and it's generally positive when it has a brown sign dedicated to itself—usually it is an attraction. I am not disappointed—a nice walk through the grounds, which contributes to my mileage target and the destination is a lovely, 'stately home' type hotel.

Walking through the hotel grounds with the wide roads and large trees bordering the roads reminds me of our time living in Le Vesinet in Paris. We lived on a wide avenue with big trees bordering the avenue for two and a half years when I joined Lexmark. Mind you, we very nearly did not go as a few weeks before we left the UK, James who was only 6 at the time had a problem one day at school with his balance. It took a while to be diagnosed, and it was a very worrying time.

During the day at school, he had fallen over a few times and kept veering to his left—after many tests whilst staying in hospital it transpired that he had a stroke, which you normally associate with elderly people certainly not a 6-year-old. Anne stayed in the hospital with James, and I looked after Matthew at home. I do remember explaining to him, that James and Mummy were in hospital and asked him whether he had any questions. "Yes," Matthew responded and proceeded to ask me a question about the difference between automatic cars and cars with manual gears.

Most amusing at a time of high angst. Fortunately, we did move, and James had excellent treatment via French doctors and physios although his left leg has since always been thinner than his right—albeit still twice the girth of one of my pins!

We all loved the time in Paris—it is amazing how popular we became with our English friends as we were a very convenient stopping point for them when travelling from the UK to Europe. Tim and his family were in Brussels at this time, which was only a 3-hour drive away so we would meet up regularly. The boys picked up the French language quickly (although just as quickly lost it again when we moved back to the UK), Anne is fluent and navigated herself around very well, and I had lessons, which enabled me to order a beer at least. The food was like something from another world. Visiting Carrefour to look at the vegetable and fish displays was an experience as the impressive displays were vibrant, and colourful.

We had a lovely patisserie just at the end of our road and a weekend treat involved the purchase of lemon tarts for Anne, me, and any visitors with a sweet tooth. We spent a lot of our income on the rental for a large house—it was a good decision because we had a lot of gear and with James's health scare, we were unable to declutter our stuff in advance of our relocation. So, we had a big spacious house with seven bedrooms, study, dining room, a basement, and a wine cellar.

It was like a large holiday home with marble floors and lots of space to play hide and seek. The basement became a social hub when our friends would come round to play table tennis—the ceiling was a bit low, but I could still smash the ball when required. Anne, in particular, enjoyed her time in Paris and was disappointed when we did return to the UK. Anne had a routine of French lessons, frequent coffee mornings, helping at school and French conversation groups, did weekly wine tasting and cooking classes. We went skiing, visited Rome, Geneva, and Monaco to name but a few cities, hosted friends and family, and in hindsight, the 2½ years really flew past.

The sun literally comes out as I arrive at the hotel and when I see the tepees at the front of the hotel I tentatively wonder if this is where I will find my bed for the evening. Vince, the manager of the hotel has kindly donated bed and breakfast—and I am relieved to find my bed is inside the hotel. It is a shame I did not bring my swimming trunks as the hotel has a pool; on the other hand, it would not have been fair to expose my feet to the other guests (I am thinking along the lines of the soundtrack of Jaws as my feet break the surface of the water with similar scary accompanying theme music).

I enjoy a couple of drinks in the bar and then have a bizarre chance encounter walking past the dining room towards reception. I happen to glance into the room while Helen, who was my peer as HR director at Jewson several years ago glances out—of all the places in the world and what a coincidence. Helen is dining with her family and kindly donates to the cause while we have a catch-up. Vince, the manager of the hotel unexpectedly donates my evening meal as well, so all in all an excellent day.

News Headlines Context, 15 October 2020

In news headlines, Boris Johnson has been warned not to extend Brexit negotiations any further as the Prime Minister gives the European Union an extra 24 hours. Last month, the Prime Minister gave the EU up until today to secure a post-Brexit trade deal with the UK in order to allow plenty of time for an agreement to be ratified by the end of the transition period in December. Keyless car technology is blamed for a dramatic rise in thefts across these major UK cities. Keyless car technology accounts for a greater proportion of claims as thefts have increased by 20% over the past four years. The trick works using relay devices, which can trick nearby vehicles into thinking that the owner's key is nearby and unlock the car.

Coronavirus Daily Context, 15 October 2020

"Manchester lockdown revolt: Tory MPs team up with Andy Burnham in stinging attack on Boris. Manchester Mayor Andy Burnham was joined by Tory MPs as northern politicians lashed out at the Government's 'flawed and unfair' plan to put the city region under tier three lockdown. Coronavirus testing took one step further in the UK today, as Oxford University scientists announced they had developed an all-new test for the virus. When can you get one? Oxford University scientists today announced they had developed a new test for COVID-19, which dramatically cuts down the time it takes to receive results. Academics at the university's Department of Physics developed the diagnostic test, which can detect the virus in just five minutes. They claim the test retains high levels of

accuracy despite the dramatic reduction in testing time, but it won't become available for some time."

Tracking new cases 18,440; deaths 151
(Source: coronavirus.data.gov.uk)

It is great during such a challenging climate that Oxford is at the forefront of developing testing and vaccines—hopefully being part of the ultimate solution. I could do with Andy Burnham and Boris continuing to discuss the specifics of the planned Manchester lockdown for a few more weeks.

River Wear.

Great wall design—Tudhoe.

Halloween decorations—Tudhoe.

Sign for Redworth Hall.

Redworth Hall approach.

Tepees on the grounds.

Me arriving.

Fantastic and very comfortable room.

Bit of a treat.

Six Days Before Arriving at Milestone Three

Day 33. Friday 16 October, Redworth Hall to Richmond

I am a bit disappointed to be leaving Redworth today—maybe Anne and I will return at a later date for a weekend break. I walk over 18 miles today and through some beautiful countryside. I have now walked 312 miles, so I am over halfway. I have a particularly enjoyable and kind of retro lunch at the White Swan in Gilling West. It is nice enough to sit outside and have a fish finger sandwich for the first time in years. The owners kindly donate the sandwich and coffee, which is highly appreciated.

I come across an impressive stack of hay rolls as you can see from the photo below. It cannot be easy to stack them so neatly, and it could be fun to use it as a giant game of outdoor Jenga. The best game of Jenga I ever played was on our wedding day, funnily enough. I cannot recall how it happened but 'the boys' led by my best man Jeremy and myself organised a game in the bar before the reception started.

We had around 10 of us playing, and there was an incentive   the loser had to buy drinks for the group playing. The tension mounted; the tower wobbled precariously several times. It went extremely high (nearly up to Tim's height although not up to mine) until a huge crash echoed around the bar as the individual bricks tumbled onto the hotel coffee table. Thanks, Jeremy—mine will be a pint of lager, please.

It is interesting to note the different sights that you come across—one homeowner has built a scarecrow called 'Kindness' in their garden, and I come across a sign for a blacksmith, which I do not recall ever seeing in my life before! I am staying with Paul and Ros again tonight hence why I am aiming for Richmond where one of them will collect me as part of the school run collection pick up.

I have some time in Richmond, which seems a genuinely nice town, most of the coffee shops are full but I come across a tea shop with an available table, and

I have a delicious Bakewell tart. It is nice to be back at Paul's (although I am not sure George thinks the same as he gives up his room again) and we have a Chinese takeaway banquet followed by the final episodes of the Mandalorian. I may have to sign up for Disney+ in order to watch series two when it is released.

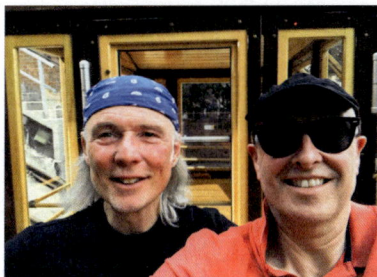

Jeremy. "It was my pleasure to play the best man role for Dave when asked and had a deep well of great shared experiences to call upon come speech time. Many joyous and unforgettable episodes and adventures came to mind (and remain crystal clear to this day!) as we kicked off our careers in the commercial world at Black & Decker, side by side in our respective Vauxhall Cavaliers and armed with loaded Topper cases full of irresistible deals for our unsuspecting customers!"

News Headlines Context, 16 October 2020

In news headlines, Brexit ultimatum: Barnier told don't come to London unless EU budges—'no basis' for talks.

Boris Johnson's chief Brexit negotiator has told Michel Barnier there is 'no basis' for Brexit trade talks unless he dramatically changes his position. In a phone call this afternoon, Lord Frost warned his EU counterpart wrangling over the future relationship pact won't resume until the bloc agrees to discuss legal texts on a daily basis for the next two weeks.

Their discussion comes after Boris Johnson walked out of the negotiations, leaving Brussels with one final opportunity to avoid a no-deal Brexit. Disney puts racism warning on classics Peter Pan, Dumbo and more 'wrong then, wrong now'.

Disney has strengthened its racism warnings before classic films like 'Peter Pan' and 'The Jungle Book' on its streaming service. The disclaimer reads: "Rather than remove this content, we want to acknowledge its harmful impact, learn from it and spark conversation to create a more inclusive future together. Disney is committed to creating stories with inspirational and aspirational themes that reflect the rich diversity of the human experience around the globe."

Coronavirus Daily Context, 16 October 2020

Coronavirus map: R rate between 1.3 and 1.5 as Boris issues grave update in the briefing. The UK's coronavirus reproduction.

(R) number has increased across the country, according to the latest government figures. Boris Johnson has been urged to introduce an immediate national circuit breaker lockdown to reduce the spread of coronavirus, as leading scientists warn the new three-tier system does not go far enough. Independent SAGE, a group of scientists who provide scientific advice about coronavirus, has backed a nationwide circuit breaker lockdown that would replicate the measures put in place at the start of the pandemic.

"The lockdown would last for 2-3 weeks and would lead to the closure of schools, universities, non-essential retail and businesses, leisure and hospitality sectors. The panel of expert scientists, chaired by former chief scientific adviser Sir David King, has set out a "six-week emergency plan" to bring infection rates below 5,000 a day. They argue the Government's three-tier system does not go far enough to reverse the current surge in cases."

Tracking new cases 17,727; deaths 147

(Source: coronavirus.data.gov.uk)

I watched the film *Contagion* while I had my unscheduled two-week hiatus for feet recovery. Considering the film was made in 2011, it's uncanny how many parallels there are to the situation today, and there is a great description as to what the R number means as well. Boris could have used a clip from the film to explain this to the masses. A national circuit breaker is a big worry.

It would mean the end of my trek. I must hope that if it happens then it is planned a couple of weeks ahead—or maybe I will have to up my mileage again with the risk to my feet that entails. The death rate is now approaching 150 and the infection rate approaching twenty thousand, so something must be done differently.

It feels selfish of me to hope that a circuit breaker is not introduced; after all, people's lives and families are being disrupted by this; on the other hand, while part of this walk is for my own challenge, the larger part is to raise funds to help others. If I do not complete the walk but still meet the fund-raising target, then that is still a failure in my eyes. I need to finish the 600 miles to be able to say to myself 'job done'.

Breakfast fuel with charity tin.

Redworth sunrise.

Giant Jenga game for outdoors.

Kindness in Piercebridge.

Rare sign—blacksmiths!

Fish finger sandwich!

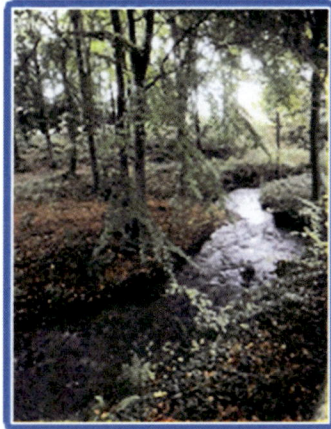

Aske.

Five Days Before Arriving at Milestone Three

Day 34. Saturday 17 October, Carthorpe to Leyburn

I am excited to be walking in the Yorkshire Dales but also a little apprehensive as I know there will be some 'hills' coming my way, and I now have the 85-litre backpack with me for the foreseeable future. I leave a few clothes behind for Paul to kindly post on at some point. It is a wet start, but it soon clears up. No coffee shops but a combination of jelly babies and Soreen slices, which remind me of malt loaf snacks after school, keep my energy levels high.

The walk is just under 17 miles and the views are fantastic, I can certainly feel the inclines in my calves, but the bigger climbs are still ahead of me, I think. More fun sights today include a house that had a kennel for the electronic lawnmower—and the owners have even given it a name. It is probably cheaper to run than having a dog although not so much fun taking it for a walk. I also enjoy watching the farmer with his sheepdog herding the sheep from one end of the field to the other and seeing it live rather than on a screen in the days of 'One man and his dog' on television. There must be some learning here to be applied to attempt herding young children to go in the chosen direction.

I come across a teashop that offers unusual food combinations in their sandwiches—I go for cheese with apple toasted sandwich, which is delicious. I have a lovely room at Eastfield Lodge, which along with breakfast is kindly donated by Henry and Penny. Henry used to live close to where I grew up in Buntingford and Penny is working in the charity business where she takes teams on walking adventures abroad (great job).

They are a lovely couple; I already plan to go back to the Dales again and will definitely stay there—and pay for it naturally. Fortunately, I arrive in good time because my portable charger flashes in the room while charging my phone and blows a fuse—the shops are still open, and I can buy a replacement. Imagine if it had happened in one of the remote locations with no shops nearby, and I could no longer charge my phones up .... I break out in a cold sweat just thinking about it.

News Headlines Context, 17 October 2020

In news headlines, Bed bugs: A home remedy could deter the creepy crawlies from infesting your home. Bed bugs feed on human blood during the night. While seemingly a thing of nightmares, they're very real. How can you deter them from infesting your bedroom? Leaving itchy bite marks on your skin, the thought of these bugs feeding on your flesh at night can creep anybody out. Known as Cimex Lectularius, according to Pest Smart Control, bed bugs can range from 1 mm to 7 mm in size.

One plant-based essential oil could ward them off. One of the best essential oils to deter bed bugs from settling in your bedroom is lemongrass. World record set for shortest EVER time measurement—'247 zeptoseconds.' Scientists have set a remarkable new world record for the shortest time ever measured, a duration requiring a new category. A team of atomic physicists led by Goethe University's Professor Reinhard Dörner have recorded the smallest time period, beating the previous recordholder, which was measured in femtoseconds. To achieve this, the team of scientists measured how long it takes for a photon to cross a hydrogen molecule—and came up with a new timeframe.

Coronavirus Daily Context, 17 October 2020

Coronavirus breakthrough: Scientists say one million per day to be tested before Christmas. Scientists have said up to one million people per day could be tested for coronavirus by Christmas with results in just 15 minutes. During a press conference on Friday, Prime Minister Boris Johnson said new tests were 'faster, simpler and cheaper'.

"He said: 'We are now testing more people than any other country in Europe, but we always want to go further. Scientists and companies in Britain and around the world have been developing new tests, which are faster, simpler and cheaper. To help support your wellbeing during this trying time, Mind—a mental health charity—has shared its top tips for spending more time indoors.

Home is meant to be a haven, so it's important to find ways to relax. Some creative activities to try, including drawing, painting, collage, sewing or upcycling. Unwind by meditating, yoga or listening to music; perhaps DIY or colouring is more your thing? Whether you are working from home or not, putting into place a visible routine may be helpful. Keeping a consistent routine, as well as waking up and going to bed at the same time is recommended."

Tracking new cases 14,767; deaths 176

(Source: coronavirus.data.gov.uk)

Some interesting tips to help deal with the mental health impact of the virus. For me, the home 'safe haven' is not truly relevant at the moment, but the consistent routine certainly is—also I go to bed and get up at very similar times albeit the bed itself is different every night. I also listen to music throughout the day (Heart radio usually unless there is a football match on radio 5 live) and I struggle to sew on missing buttons let alone create something new. I remember distinctly at primary school that the teacher would not help me thread my needle, and I spent the whole lesson trying to do that unsuccessfully. Mentally I have never recovered.

Snape Castle.

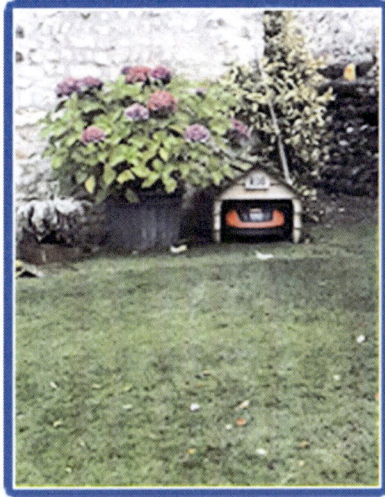

Rob the electric lawnmower pet.

Live 'One man and his dog' show.

Four Days Before Arriving at
Milestone Three

Day 35. Sunday 18 October, Leyburn to Starbotton

Today is the most enjoyable day of walking that I have done so far. I am hardly on the roads at all and the views from the bridleways across the Yorkshire Dales are spectacular. As you will see from the photos below, I even practice the 'panoramic' setting feature. There is hardly a soul around, and I know if I had had my 4-year-old niece, 2-year-old nephew, or 22-year-old sons with me they would particularly have enjoyed splashing in the puddles en-route.

Once I get back on the roads again later in the day the number of motorbikes is noticeable (I had been warned). The elevation in terms of height today is 1898 feet—much higher than previous days unsurprisingly. It is amusing to see a small shop called Arkwrights although it was not on a corner so it could not be the premises from "Open All Hours".

The walking over the Dales and some of the spectacular views remind me of the Jewson Jaunts that I did with the Jewson executive team a few years ago. We did two Jaunts as I recall—one in Scotland and one in Wales—with the intention of raising funds for our charity partners, which we did, but we achieved so much more than purely fund-raising. Led by our boss Peter, they proved to be fantastic team bonding events. Lasting for around a week we paid for our own expenses and were able to raise decent sums for Macmillan I think it was then.

Different members played different roles in the team, Bill was the lead navigator and Mike, who became a close friend, was the medic, minibus driver and my partner in crime for having fun. For the walk-in Scotland, we stayed in less than salubrious accommodation, but they served good beer at the end of the day and with the influence of Simon the youngest team member we evolved into drinking Jaeger bombs in the bar during the early hours. I probably did not have the most appropriate clothes selection with me (although I learned for the second year) as I went walking in shorts and with a straw hat to keep the sun off my head, earning the nickname of 'Benidorm' from Mike.

Frank, the sales director struggled most with his feet and had multiple blisters from day one. He had also brought about five or six pairs of boots, trainers etc and changed his footwear two or three times a day but to no avail. He became christened as 'shoes'.

On one of the walks, we got lost and ended up traipsing through some fields. We sent Charlie our resident Scot to discuss our location with a local farmer who we saw in a neighbouring field. He did not understand a word that Charlie said, however, as he was a Cockney landowner living in Scotland. Our amusement was compounded when Vince the Operations Director leaned on the metal fence to listen to the conversation—suddenly recoiling as the shock from the electric fence went through his body. Very amusing.

The walk in the following year in Wales was along the coastal path and less hilly as I recall. There were several amusing incidents. Starting when it transpired on the first night that Mike and I were sharing a bathroom although did not realise so at the time fortunately, I had finished in the shower as he strode in to use the facilities. I also did not have far to walk when one night as I relieved myself of the previous night's lager consumption around 3:00 a.m. Mike was sprawled across his bed, his bedroom door open and the TV blaring until I pressed the off button, closed his door and returned to my room to try and sleep.

In the evening, we would congregate for beer and stories, which was always a highlight. In the bar, one evening, Mike and Peter were deep in a work conversation while we drank our beers. Always on the lookout for an opportunity, I noticed a couple of signs behind where Peter and Mike were sitting—the premises specialised also in weddings—and one of the signs spelt out LOVE. It helped create a very moving photograph, which I was able to exploit appropriately.

Mike also updated us regularly on what he got up to while driving the van and the rest of us were walking. One day, he knocked on the door of a coffee shop in the village, entered the hallway and asked for a cup of tea and cake. It was however not a café but just a regular homeowner very bemused why this strange man had entered his residential premises and requested refreshment. We were crying with laughter when Mike recounted the tale later that day. He had also wanted to use the toilet but had not dared to ask.

Mike makes me look like a technological whizz kid, so I always enjoyed having him around. He is the only man I have known who, when using a projector to display his presentation, managed to invert the projected slides so they were upside down. He did this twice in one day. I have never seen it before or afterwards.

Mind you everybody likes Mike—he is also the only man I know who received a standing ovation from over a thousand attendees at the Jewson conference when he announced his retirement. We meet once or twice every year with our respective 'support teams' to keep the banter exchanges going.

I walk 18 miles all the way through today—I do call in at a pub as I near my destination and see what looks like a tremendous roast dinner coming out on a plate, but unfortunately, the place is full and appropriately following social distancing restrictions. It is a good job I planned accommodation ahead at the Fox and Hounds (thanks for the discounted rate) in Starbotton as there are so few pubs around and certainly no coffee shops.

I really enjoyed my stay at the Fox and Hounds—I have a lovely room, there is a welcoming log fire in the bar and the food is tasty and filling. The manager is very hospitable and arranges for me to have a continental breakfast so that I can make a quick getaway the next day.

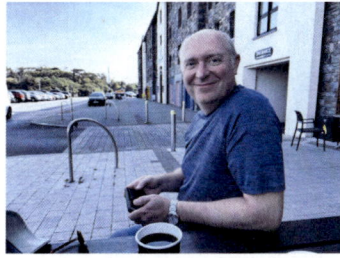

Andrew: David was very buoyant through the day; great views and he was always bringing the conversations around to the target of a pub at the end of the day's walks. I asked if he knew whether they did pork scratchings and was alarmed but he had not got his Support Team to find out. I suggested he called Anne immediately to find out but for some reason David was not as confident as me that this was a good idea. I even suggested a backup plan of calling into a news agent and buying a bag ahead just in case the pub didn't serve them. I was equally alarmed when I called him upon arrival that this backup plan hadn't been executed either. Maybe I price them more than he does, but I know that's not true either. Perhaps this walking and time to think must be making other priorities come to the forefront.

News Headlines Context, 18 October 2020

In news headlines, SpaceX: Elon Musk claims the Starship Mars mission has a 'fighting chance' of flying in 4 YEARS. SpaceX Starship could be ready for its first trip to Mars as early as 2024, the pioneering rocket company's CEO Elon Musk has claimed. SpaceX is reportedly on schedule to be ready to launch its revolutionary Starship on an unmanned mission to Mars in 2024, Elon Musk has revealed to the International Mars Society Convention. Speaking with Mars Society founder Robert Zubrin, Mr Musk said: "I think we have a fighting chance of making that second Mars transfer window."

China places new missiles on the border as fears Beijing is 'stepping up war preparations'. China is building its military forces on its southeast coast in preparations for a possible invasion of Taiwan, military analysts have said. The People's Liberation Army has been upgrading its missile bases on the coast that faces the island nation of Taiwan. A China-based military source said the country had deployed its advanced hypersonic missile the DF-17 to the coastal region.

Coronavirus Daily Context, 18 October 2020

Coronavirus update: Public Health England warns Calpol could 'mask' COVID-19 coronavirus has three flagship warning signs: a high temperature, a new, continuous cough and/or a change or loss to a person's sense of smell or taste. Yet Calpol could 'mask' the virus. Two areas of England are currently under Tier 3 restrictions, the harshest currently in place—but even these do not amount to a full lockdown, with schools still open and hospitality venues limited but still able to serve customers.

"The UK's R number—the number of people each coronavirus case infects—has increased from between 1.2 and 1.5 the previous week to between 1.3 and 1.5 in the most recent week, according to official figures. There are no current plans for the UK to go back into lockdown, as the Prime Minister insists that is not a move he wants to make as the UK charts itself through the coronavirus crisis. Westminster is sticking to its guns and following the planned regional restrictions method—although the results of this method remain to be seen. Mr Johnson has said that he would not hesitate to put further measures in place if infection rates did not begin to tail off."

Tracking new cases 14,189; deaths 159

(Source: coronavirus.data.gov.uk)

I am not sure what further measures could be now other than full lockdown as the numbers just continue going up and the loudness of the rhetoric seems to be on a similar growth curve.

Leyburn.

Sunrise in Leyburn.

Waterfall Wensley.

River Ure.

Arkwrights (not corner shop!)

Walden.

Newbiggin.

Newbiggin

Bishopdale.

Bishopdale.

17% hill decline—Buckden.

Buckden.

Starbotton.

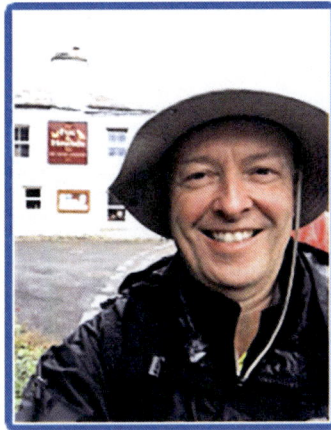

Arrival at Fox & Hounds.

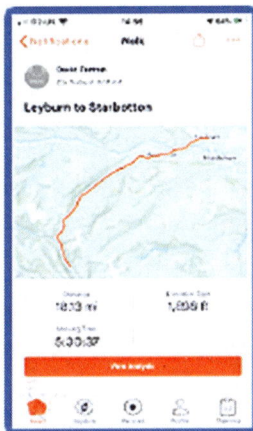

Strava Summary.

Three Days Before Arriving at Milestone Three

Day 36. Monday 19 October, Starbotton to Skipton

I rummage through the fifteen or so pockets in my rucksack today to find the sun cream, although 30 minutes after applying it, the sun disappears again. I am managing OK with the larger rucksack on my back, which is great as there is no support team, and I have not used taxis to transport it since my first week's walk. It is such a great feeling to discover a pub at exactly right the point of the day for a caffeine hit and catch up on emails.

In the middle of my walk in one of the noticeably quiet areas, I come across a school—it looks like one building only, with a football pitch next door. What a fantastic location for a school. School is so fundamental to creating the person you turn out to be—along with family. Many of the core skills you develop in later life have their foundations in the early years.

Leadership is an area that really interests me, and which applies both in a work and school setting. You are increasingly given responsibility at school whether you are into academic studies, playing a sport, a musician, or a thespian then you get opportunities to lead and develop others as well as yourself.

I really like the definition of leadership from John Quincy Adams, "If your actions inspire others to dream more, learn more, do more and become more, you are a leader." If you are successful in inspiring your subordinates, you can easily overcome any current and future challenge easily. As I look back on my career, I have led teams whether formally or informally from day one, and I have also been led by numerous leaders. What I have applied to my style is to set ambitious goals and try to inspire the team to attain them.

From the feedback that I have had over the years, I believe it is one of my strengths—to show interest in what the individuals in your team are doing, to give them space to grow and make mistakes and to encourage them through questions and reflection on what they can do better and how. Leadership is not easy and while I have led many teams I would say only once have I truly created a high performing team. In my definition, this is when the sum of the parts is stronger than the individual components or team members in isolation.

At Jewson, I had key skilled, motivated individuals as my reports who in their areas of specialism were stronger than me, who would challenge and support each other as well as myself, and where we achieved the stretch goals that had been set. I launched a graduate programme to deliver succession planning into the marketing function and to bring new skills into the broader team also, which I was immensely proud of. In fact, when I look back at the teams I have led, I am most proud of the fine leaders that many have turned into and keep in touch with several of them.

So, what qualities make up a strong leader? For me, the leader has a clear sense of purpose and direction, can inspire, and excite the team members to raise their game, is able to challenge and coach the individuals and sub-teams, celebrates success and never rests—always raising the bar. It is a key skill of the leader also to know when to release team members (as they have ambitions of their own) whilst executing a succession plan to keep the team alive and growing—replacing those that leave and evolving the team dynamics. My role model for a leader would be Sir Alex Ferguson.

I have read his books, and he is inspirational regarding consistent delivery of results while regenerating three or four 'high-performing' teams. In his autobiography, "Sir Alex", the success at United is attributed to his 'vision, energy, and ability that he was able to build teams both on and off the pitch'. Agility and looking ahead are key attributes of a successful leader. Sir Alex talks about defeats sometimes being the best outcomes—'to react to adversity is a quality' and while nobody chooses to lose, everybody does at some stage. What separates great leaders from good or good leaders from bad is how that loss is utilised, leveraged, and built upon.

I have a horrible experience today when it feels that the whole walk could be at risk as the virus threatens to beat me. I take a phone call from the manager at the Crown in Colne where I am staying in 2 days' time. He asks whether I still plan on staying there?—of course, I do—he then reveals that the night I plan to stay there is their final night open before they close due to the local virus lockdown directive. Phew! One day later and I could not have stayed—the closest shave so far.

I struggle to find independent accommodation tonight, so I have ended up in a Travelodge at Skipton for tonight and tomorrow (rest day). The Travelodge is handily located next door to a farm shop and a Burger King—so farm shop picnic tonight and Burger King special on the rest day tomorrow. Just under 17 miles today, and I think the lower mileage per day compared to the first week is clearly helping my feet (no blister problems touch wood).

News Headlines Context, 19 October 2020

In news headlines, Not good enough! David Frost demands EU offers more despite Barnier's last-minute shift. Brussels must move further before Brexit trade talks can resume, Boris Johnson's chief negotiator today warned. Lord Frost insisted there was still 'no basis' for new negotiations despite Michel Barnier's offer to intensify the negotiations and work on a legal text setting out the terms of a deal. Downing Street said talks between the pair were 'constructive' but insisted there must be a 'fundamental change' in approach from the European Union. Russia warning: Vladimir Putin panics as the nation braces for a population slump of 1.2 million.

Russia's population could decline by 1.2 million people by 2024—with President Vladimir Putin already putting measures in place to face up against the looming crisis. This year the population of Russia is due to decrease by 352,000 people and President Vladimir Putin hopes to resolve the issue. In July, Mr Putin tasked the federal government to implement immigration policies that will ensure sustainable population growth by 2030. This year's slump in the population is the worst since 2006 and has been blamed on a mixture of falling births, a decline in immigration, and the coronavirus pandemic.

Coronavirus Daily Context, 19 October 2020

"Prime Minister Boris Johnson has repeatedly said he does not want to put the UK into a second lockdown following the economic repercussions of the first lockdown, which began in March this year. Each of the devolved nations has diverged significantly from the central government's advice and have carved individual paths through the crisis. Greater Manchester leaders and the Government are locked in a bitter showdown over placing the area into stricter lockdown measures. But will Manchester go into lockdown?"

I see both perspectives in the dispute about putting Greater Manchester into tier 3. I think Andy Burnham is right to push the government on behalf of his constituents however, it is unrealistic to expect the government to pay more than for those living in Liverpool for example. So, compromise is needed by Andy Burnham or Boris should be more directive in his approach.

Starbotton sunrise.

Fantastic location—Starbotton school.

Kettlewell.

Hawkswick

Hawkswick.

Kilnsey.

Arrival at Travelodge Skipton.

Healthy DIY Breakfast.s

R&R.

Caffeine at next door farm shop.

Two Days Before Arriving at Milestone Three

Day 38. Wednesday 21 October, Skipton to Colne

I feel good after my rest day and have a relatively gentle walk just over 12 miles today—that puts me at 375 miles and 241 to go. Most of the elevations are behind me, I hope. I find a great source of supply for our Christmas tree this year, but unfortunately, there is literally no room in my rucksack (probably not even for donated beers). Christmas is one of those fantastic times of the year—I love it.

Even more than my summer holiday, which is one of my other highlights, Christmas is a time when most people are off, and my previous businesses have largely closed over the period so there are few emails coming through. Traditionally we are not able to put up the decorations until after the boys' birthday on 16 December but ideally, I would put them all up in early December.

To me, Christmas means time with family, lovely food, my favourite meal (if I am ever on Death Row, then Christmas dinner would be my last meal), good TV and games. I love to watch a James Bond film at Christmas and especially if there is a new one released. This stems back to when we would visit Grandma at Christmas and then go to visit my aunt and uncle for the evening. We would debate what to watch—my cousin Steph pushed for the Muppets or Top of the Pops, and I always wanted Bond—usually, I won as I was the guest.

As a youngster, it is all about the presents and then at some point of maturity, it becomes the food and the experience itself, which is the highlight. I enjoy visiting others and having parents visit us. I do not enjoy the preparation however as the cleaning is a major task and unfortunately, I am reasonably competent at this. I should have taken a lead from Ben Fogle's advice in his book *The Wilderness Years*, which is a great read. He talks about the male secret where a boy/man purposely does a task they hate doing badly, in order to avoid having to do it again in the future. I absolutely can relate to this.

The ideal Christmas day for me is cold outside, playing family games in the morning, opening the presents, with some finger food and a bottle of fizz. To be followed by Christmas snacks and beer/wine (I am flexible) and then eat the Christmas meal around 4:00 p.m. This has changed over the years as we used to enjoy it around 2:00 p.m. so that we could fit a cold buffet in later, however, we are now prepared to delay the buffet until Boxing day.

The main meal is turkey, roast potatoes, sprouts, parsnips, carrots, lots of stuffing, bread sauce, lots of gravy, pigs in blankets (loads of them) followed by trifle or Christmas pudding and cheese and biscuits. Wine during the meal and Baileys or port to follow with chocolates. I am drooling now. If we have people over, we may play more games (charades is another favourite) or watch a film. Films are tricky as they need to balance the interests of various age brackets.

My vote only counts now, at best, as one of four, so Bond days are largely historical. We try to watch Christmas films the week prior to the day as part of the exciting build-up. I love National Lampoons Christmas vacation whereas the other three family members are a little bored with it.

Anne and I have tried to persuade the boys to watch *It's a Wonderful Life*, however, they refuse to watch any film before around 2010 as the special effects will not be up to scratch so we have no chance with a black and white film. We usually compromise on safe classics such as Elf, Cheaper by the Dozen, Miracle on 34th street. I forgot the present opening. When the kids were young it was around 6:00 a.m.; now they have matured, 11:00 a.m. is acceptable. Oh, and an open fire (recently converted to a wood burner).

My photos have not done justice to the views, and I do not think the grey weather helped either. I arrive early afternoon in Colne and have time for a soup and a sandwich kindly donated by a furnishing shop that had a cafeteria section. I receive more tips, which are very much appreciated. Just make it in time to the Crown at Colne as due to local lockdown they close from tonight. Thanks to the manager for donating bed and breakfast.

News Headlines Context, 21 October 2020

In news headlines, Brexit talks to restart: Boris accepts EU capitulation after Barnier humiliating defeat. Boris Johnson agreed to restart Brexit talks tonight after the European Union caved on his demands to compromise. Michel Barnier finally admitted defeat in his battle to keep Britain tied to Brussels in a last-ditch bid to salvage the wrangling over an EU-UK future relationship pact. He agreed to travel to London tomorrow for showdown talks with UK counterpart Lord Frost and has declared a deal by mid-November is within reach. The pair agreed to meet after Mr Barnier reassured the Prime Minister's chief negotiator of the concessions during an hour-long phone call. Britain has been 'naive' in dealing with China and Russia's threats—Urgent warning issued. Chinese and Russian threats have not been dealt with adequately, former Cabinet Secretary, Lord Mark Sedwill has warned. Russian and Chinese state actors have been accused of launching cyber-attacks on the UK. Amid these threats, the former civil servant warned Britain had been 'naïve' in dealing with the two states.

Lord Sedwill, who served as Cabinet Security and National Security Adviser, under Boris Johnson and Theresa May, also claimed the West needs a strong America to lead the Western alliance.

Coronavirus Daily Context, 21 October 2020

"Coronavirus vaccine: the UK could soon be in 'reasonable position'— SAGE expert gives update Speaking today, professor John Edmunds, from the London School of Hygiene & Tropical Medicine, stated the UK 'could be in a reasonable' position in the coming months. With the second wave of the virus taking hold across the country, professor Edmunds stated a successful vaccine could soon put the UK in a better position. During a session of the Science and Technology and Health and Social Care Committee, professor Edmunds stated the Vaccine Taskforce had been smart to invest in six different possible drugs. Greater Manchester will be subjected to Tier 3 coronavirus restrictions from Friday following more than a week of failed negotiations on financial support between the Government and local leaders."

Tracking new cases 25,454; deaths 222
(Source: coronavirus.data.gov.uk)

Not a surprise that Greater Manchester will go into Tier 3 from Friday. This could well affect one of my overnight stops so will develop my plan B as I am due to stay over with my cousin Julie. I only just made it yesterday in Colne— one day's delay, and I would have had nowhere to stay.

Leeds & Liverpool canal.

Christmas trees in Lothersdale.

Thornton-in-Craven.

One Day Before Arriving at Milestone Three

Day 39. Thursday 22 October, Colne to Ramsbottom

I exchange a bit of banter this morning with my breakfast statue companions Laurel and Hardy and thanks for a lovely full English breakfast to boost my calorie intake. This is one of those depressing days when I just want to get to my destination—the Eagle & Child at Ramsbottom. It rains pretty well the whole journey, so I am not sure that I see Burnley or Nelson in their best light (if there is one). I am absolutely drenched, and it is that horrible constant and very wet drizzle.

Everything is so dull and grey, and this is definitely one of my 'low' days. On the positive side (because there always is one), I have a pavement to walk for the entire 17 miles so do not need to keep my wits about me, in case I have to dive into the verge to avoid the oncoming lorries. This trip is proving very educational—I have never seen a sign with the word "panopticon" before until today. It's defined as 'a circular prison with cells arranged around a central well, from which prisoners could at all times be observed'. I did not actually see the tree panopticon but in my mind, I can see a clear arrangement of vertical branches forming a barrier to entrance or exit.

I walk sadly past a funeral cortege mid-morning coming from the opposite direction like a line of ants marching towards their destination as determined by the navigator ant. Ants apparently use visual landmarks and let their stomachs guide their way when they set off on their march—I guess there is some similarity in that there is generally food and refreshment available at funerals although I never feel like eating at them. I hate funerals.

I reflect that I am probably lucky to have only attended a handful or so, although my attendance is inevitably only going to go in one direction. My first one was Grandma's back in 2003. Tim was working in Brussels and could not attend, Andrew and I travelled with our cousins in the hearse. Tears flowed. Mum was particularly brave.

I could not help thinking briefly, as the coffin disappeared after the service, of the Bond film *Diamonds Are Forever* when Bond was knocked unconscious and lying in a burning coffin. Unfortunately, Grandma did not have possession of the missing diamonds so there was no dramatic escape. Both of my aunts have passed away, along with a work colleague a few years ago. If there is a positive that comes from these events it is the opportunity to see relations, friends that you have not seen for several years and to provide support to the family members.

It is only a small comfort, however. By far the worst—by which I mean most emotional—funeral that I attended was for somebody that I never even met. Paul and Ros lost Edward (a twin) within a few days of the birth; fortunately, George survived. To see Paul carrying such a small coffin in front of him and with the dignity that he showed was something that I will never forget. Also, with it being so close to home with regard to our boys going into special care when they were born—reiterating the importance of supporting others at a critical life stage.

I have now walked 392 miles and all being well then, in two weeks today I will cross the finish line. I am very appreciative to the Eagle and Crown for donating bed and breakfast. The room is fantastic—one of the best so far—and the lovely high-powered shower just makes everything so much better. The Eagle and Crown was the Community Pub Award winner in 2014 and 2015 and has some lovely unique touches.

For example, there is a fridge in my room with fruit, chilled water, and a couple of locally made delicious yoghurts. I have a lovely meal in the restaurant in front of a log burning fire (this gives the platform for a wonderful night for me). I meet the lady who does the social media for the Eagle & Child and has kindly publicised my activity on their social channels.

The Eagle & Child have a policy of offering opportunities to youngsters and giving them a chance—I love that as it touches so many buttons for me. They focus their recruitment on young people aged 16-25 who are not in education, employment, or training, to support them into an apprenticeship and career pathway. A lovely stay in a lovely pub with lovely food.

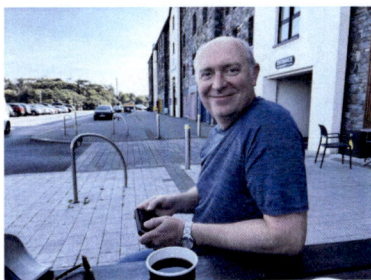

Andrew: Bad weather meant I called him slightly more than normal and would call his other phone if he did not answer the first one. Sometimes he would pick up and the reward was some good banter from his brother. He did not pick up as often through the day thereafter. The pub goal was definitely his goal for the day!

News Headlines Context, 22 October 2020

In news headlines, Ireland warned to brace for 'double whammy' of no-deal Brexit and coronavirus cash crisis IRELAND'S top banker has warned the country faces the bleak prospect of an economic 'double whammy' with Brexit coming on top of the financial impact of the coronavirus pandemic. Gabriel Makhlouf said Ireland would be the eurozone's biggest loser if Britain leaves the EU without a trade agreement on 31 December, with the lucrative food and agriculture sectors facing the hardest hits. The UK accounts for 38% for agricultural and food products exported from Ireland and the figure is even higher for beef.

The most played songs at funerals revealed—from Frank Sinatra to Ed Sheeran Co-op Funeralcare has released a report on the changing trends of funeral music. With music playing such a big part of life, it makes sense that it would make an appearance in death too. The songs we choose for a funeral hold a significant and personal meaning for ourselves and our loved ones. And while the reasons for these choices are unique to each person, some songs are more popular than others. 1. My Way by Frank Sinatra. To anyone who has listened to this offering by Old Blue Eyes, its place at number one won't be much of a surprise.

If ever a song encapsulates the highs and lows of a lifetime it's this. 2. Time to Say Goodbye by Andrea Bocelli and Sarah Brightman. The only classical piece on the list but one that leaves goose bumps. This beautiful duet, which is sung—for the most part—in Italian, was originally written as a farewell to boxer Henry Maske on his final match. It has since been adopted as an anthem of love and devotion to a departed loved one. 3. Over the Rainbow by Eva Cassidy. Yes, Judy Garland made the song famous but it's this version that is loved for occasion no doubt due to its reflective tone and Eva's haunting vocals.

Coronavirus Daily Context, 22 October 2020

Coronavirus: Horrifying new figures as England hospital deaths highest since May. Hospital deaths in England have now risen to levels not seen since the end of May, the latest figures have shown today. Hospital deaths in England rose to 117 on 17 October, the highest number in the country since 29 May. Of that number, 45 were reported in the North-West of England. Earlier today, Sir Patrick Vallance stated cases could be reaching up to 90,000 a day. Referencing three separate studies, the UK's chief scientific adviser highlighted the SPI-Modelling consensus, which estimates 53,000-90,000 infections a day.

"Due to this, he also warned hospital admissions will therefore rise and in turn, the R-rate will not drop. Tier 3 is the highest possible level of lockdown in the UK right now, according to the Government's new system. Ministers have resolved to introduce local mitigation against COVID-19 rather than a nationwide 'circuit breaker', heaping variable measures on top of national restrictions in some areas. As such, regions currently in Tier 2 or lower have barely tempered the virus, and may soon have to enter the highest restrictions."

Tracking new cases 23,248; deaths 234
(Source: coronavirus.data.gov.uk)

It is a tricky balance to ensure the right level of lockdown to drive down the R number whilst not suppressing more rural areas where the levels of infection are much lower. National lockdown is the harshest measure but clear, simple, and easy to communicate—the regional approach is more targeted but more complex and challenging to administer. On balance, I think the regional approach is correct whilst recognising it has issues. The death rate has shot up to nearly 250—it is frightening that the number of deaths on my second practice walk was 3!

Breakfast with Hardy.

Rain, rain.

Learning episode.

Very creative—Rawtenstall.

Eagle & Child pedigree.

Welcoming log fire in the restaurant.

Day of Arrival at Milestone Three

Day 40. Friday 23 October, Ramsbottom to Milestone 3

I mentioned yesterday the lovely touches demonstrated by the Eagle & Child, well today starts with another. Outside my door is a picnic hamper with some tasty ingredients to launch my day and to use the fresh milk that has been left in my fridge. A lovely sunrise this morning enables me to catch some unique early morning photographs.

I realise that most of the equipment that I have hired or purchased has worked well actually. The walking shoes are amazingly comfortable despite my feet issues; the waterproofs have done their job, and I have got into a seamless rhythm with the walking poles. My observations on using the walking poles: firstly, I could not do without them now—they help my posture and balance and are great for when I am walking either up or downhill. Secondly, it strikes me today just how many times one of my poles finds a small gap between flagstones on the pavement or the exceedingly small keyholes you find in a drain cover and then the pole snags out of my hands. If I were to aim for the small specific spot that it seems magnetically attracted to then I may hit it once in a hundred attempts.

A mixed day walking along the Manchester ship canal for parts of the walk. It is certainly nice to be by the canal and away from the traffic—although the sections I walk past would not let ducks get through let alone a barge. The negative aspect is that sections are closed off by locked gates and my Google Maps map does not redirect me very well. So, I get lost and waste about thirty minutes before my homing instincts kick in, and I regain the signal.

Today is fun and a sense of achievement as I am completing milestone 3— visiting the hospital where I was born and visiting the house of my maternal grandmother, which I visited many times in my youth. I think my grandmother's house is more interesting as I do not have many recollections of the hospital where I was born. 1967 was the year—2 June to be more precise that I entered the world. Number one in the charts was *Silence is Golden* by the Tremeloes.

That is certainly relevant for most of the miles that I am walking! Lassie and the Monkees were a couple of the hot TV shows. Some fantastic movie releases this year including *The Graduate*, *The Jungle Book*, *Guess Who's Coming to Dinner*, *Bonnie and Clyde*, *The Dirty Dozen*, *Valley of the Dolls*, *You Only Live Twice*, *To Sir, with Love*, *Thoroughly Modern Millie*, *Camelot*, *Cool Hand Luke* and *Casino Royale*. Since 2 June 1967, the earth has travelled approximately 873,995,227,200 miles through space.

My eyes have blinked approximately 282,298,200 times. I have taken approximately 145,665,871 steps. That is about 64,740 miles! Since this date, 20,325,470 meteors have entered the earth's atmosphere! My heart has been beaten approximately 1,976,087,400 times.

Hope Hospital is in **Pendleton, Salford**—my first landmark of milestone three. Not that I remember anything about being born there—which is actually a great relief!

From here I walk to the second landmark of Milestone Three—**May Road, Swinton**. I have not been here since 2003 when Andrew and I visited after Grandma's funeral.

I selected milestone three because Grandma was such a key figure in our lives and we spent a lot of time visiting when we were younger—and then roles reversed, and she would come to visit us.

Grandma's house looks as I remember it, although I do notice new exterior doors. I also notice how observant the neighbours are. I am approached by two different sets of neighbours to enquire if I am OK or need any help. I guess I do look a bit weird walking down a cul-de-sac with a huge rucksack and talking to myself into my phone.

I remember vividly sleeping in the bunk beds at Grandma's when we came to stay here—and having to take turns with my brother Tim to sleep in the top bunk. Fortunately, Andrew as the youngest, was way too small and always ended up sleeping in the same room as mum and dad on a camp bed. I also remember Tim and me staying with Grandma on our own for a weekend.

Whenever mum did our washing, she would check our pockets first for stones, sticks, toys etc, but I think Grandma was a little out of practice and we certainly did not think to warn her. When the washing was finished the clothes were covered in hundreds of bits of tissue paper, which needed to be individually picked off. I think that is why we then progressed to handkerchiefs.

I also walk past Grandma's flat where she moved to, on leaving May Road and that was nice because we would also often visit her there. I remember Tim and me also staying over one night at her flat. Tim left the following morning in his mud coloured mini to return to his flat in Doncaster, and Grandma and I watched him head towards the large roundabout outside her flat window. And then he came round again … and again. After the fourth or fifth time, he worked out, which exit he needed. This was pre sat nav days of course.

Grandma played a big part in our lives and loved to spend time with the family. She was the focal point for so many years enabling us to keep in touch with our cousins, while visiting Grandma. She was fiercely independent and would drive down to where we lived in her Mini even when she was well into her 80s. I remember once when Mum and Dad were away and Grandma drove to me scouts—well she had not really got to grips with hill starts, and there were lots where we lived so that was a bit of a challenge.

There was a lot of over-revving at a very steep junction followed by the car going backwards several times before we gave up and took another road. I also remember as a child, asking her to play more games of cards whenever she stayed with us and always at the very moment that she was about to depart back to Swinton—thus delaying her exit, and she would always play just one more game. She relished becoming a great grandmother when the boys were born, and her famous knitting needles were called into action producing various cardigans.

News Headlines Context, 23 October 2020

In news headlines, the Queen, Prince Charles and Prince William will sit down together within months to discuss the fate of Prince Harry and Meghan Markle in the Royal Family. On Brexit, a boost for Boris Johnson's trade deal with the EU as French fishermen have been warned to prepare for a smaller catch after Brexit. The French President Emmanuel Macron is preparing for a climbdown on his hard-line demands for access to Britain's coastal waters.

Coronavirus Daily Context, 23 October 2020

Urgent full lockdown demanded at 11th hour as experts insist Tier system 'failing'. Boris Johnson has been warned by scientists during today's Independent SAGE briefing that the nationwide tier system introduced by his

Government is failing to slow the spread of COVID-19 sufficiently. The UK has reported more than 20,000 new coronavirus cases and 200 further deaths, according to the Government's latest figures. The Prime Minister warned that an 'extreme laissez-faire' response would result in 'many thousands more deaths'.

But he insisted another lockdown was 'not the right course' for the UK, 'not when the psychological cost of lockdown is known to us, the economic cost, and not when it has been suggested that we might have to perform the same sort of brutal lockdowns again and again in the months ahead'. Mr Johnson thanked people for their 'bravery' and 'patience' in living under coronavirus restrictions. UK holidaymakers are flocking to the Canary Islands following the easing of coronavirus quarantine restrictions. Travel firms such as Tui, easyJet, Hays Travel and On the Beach reported a surge in demand since the change in Government policy was announced on Thursday night.

"Those returning from the Spanish islands no longer need to self-isolate for 14 days from 4:00 a.m. on Sunday after the destination was added to the list of travel corridors."

Tracking new cases 21,479; deaths 222
(Source: coronavirus.data.gov.uk)

It seems like two different worlds when part of the daily update raises the issue of multiple cases and deaths whilst simultaneously holidaymakers are flocking to the Canary Islands to get away from it all, albeit countries seem to go on and off the list with little notice so there could well be a sting in the tail. Tonight is the first time I have been directly affected by the virus restrictions with regard to the impact on my schedule.

I had been planning to spend the evening with my cousin Julie and husband Graeme who I have not seen for a few years but due to no household mixing in Greater Manchester as they are in tier 3 of the lockdown classification, we cancelled, and I have ended up with a room at the Premier Inn. I am disappointed as seeing Julie and Graeme was an important part of my journey, however, I rationalise to myself that it is minor in the scheme of what other people are facing. Next time maybe.

Delightful continental breakfast.

Bury.

Overgrown canal in Bury.

Salford Royal hospital (Hope).

Grandma's flat in Salford.

May Road Swinton.

Grandma's house.

Mum and Dad: Grandma thought the world of all her grandchildren, and she would have loved that you did this for charity.

Six Days Before Arriving at Milestone Four

Day 41. Saturday 24 October, Swinton to Prestbury, Macclesfield

Today I feel great as this is the start of my fourth leg of the five legs. I do not realise when I select my route on Google Maps to walk but I have a lovely surprise when I see the Man Utd Old Trafford football stadium about a mile away as I walk through Salford Quays. Walking through the Quays it is clear there has been significant investment and as I come past the ITV/BBC studios it strikes me how lucky I am to have seen such variety on my walk so far.

From busy to quiet, rural to city, scenic to busy main roads, no two days have been the same. As well as the great countryside I have really enjoyed the cities such as St Albans and Durham and I think the highlight so far for me has been the walk over the Yorkshire Dales. I am even more excited when I find myself walking up Sir Alex Ferguson Way and then find myself walking directly past the Theatre of Dreams. I am a passionate Man Utd fan and while I have been trying to block football out of my thoughts following our disappointing start to the season, it still lifts my spirits to see the magnificent stadium. It is eerily quiet. I have been to see my team around a dozen times but always on a match day when the place is heaving. Today there are only one or two loiterers, including myself.

I have been a diehard United fan since the mid-70s. I followed them as they were the nearest team to where my Grandma lived, and where I was born, so it's not a case of "following the crowd." I would not let Tim follow United as I had already chosen them. This backfired big time though. I collected at the time all the "first division" football club badges from garages when Dad bought petrol. I very generously let Tim choose his football team from this badge collection, and he chose Liverpool. I was fine with this initially, not realising they were, and remain, our biggest rivals and would continue to win championships throughout the seventies and eighties.

United in the seventies and eighties did not win the league (our 26-year famine) although we did manage to win a few FA cups. The first game I ever watched live on television was the Man Utd v Southampton FA cup final in 1976 which we lost 1-0. We did, however, come back the following season and beat Liverpool 2-1 which was doubly satisfying as it stopped them from winning a treble. It is strange now to look back to those years where you could watch one game a year live on television (the FA cup final), and today, it's wall-to-wall football.

Matthew and James rebelled against my choice of club when they were aged 5 or 6 and I was disappointed. I think for a few weeks they followed me and briefly supported Man Utd but then they were influenced by their buddies, and both became Arsenal fans. Still, it has enabled plenty of banter over the years. I had a fantastic time relishing the trophy wins during the Sir Alex Ferguson years—he is such a hero of mine for the way he turned around a struggling team from his first years in tenure to be champions multiple times in England and in Europe whilst rebuilding several different great teams during his regime.

It was great timing for him to retire and go out with our last premiership win in 2013. I can still recall vividly the greatest finish to any football match that I have seen when we beat Bayern Munich 2-1 to win the Champions league in 1999. Two goals were scored by Solskjaer and Sheringham in injury time to convert a loss into a win. I can still feel the hairs on the back of my neck when I think of that match—I leapt up from the sofa and the adrenaline surge was huge.

In recent years, since Sir Alex retired, performances and results have not been great, and it has taken me back to the drought period of the seventies and eighties with the occasional cup success. It is amazing what an impact this has on emotions. If we are doing well and beating top teams I can be on a real high, in contrast, if we lose badly or go out of a cup I can be down for a while. What is most frustrating, however, is when we are not competitive or in with a chance of winning the premiership—I can take losing, just, but it is when we are mid-table and not even close to the top teams that it becomes most depressing.

I just want hope and the chance that we can win—not for the season to be over by the halfway stage and the flame to be extinguished. Since starting this walk, United have been very inconsistent, and I have tried to block football from my mind. I have usually failed and am constantly running through the formation, team selection and transfer options in my head. I do not know how Solskjaer is ever able to switch off from it as I struggle. My mind wanders back to one of my best nights ever when I had my leaving do from Jewson. It was not best *because* I was leaving Jewson but because of the leaving do itself.

I was sad to leave colleagues and friends, but they had organised a fabulous dinner, drinks and through contacts had invited Denis Irwin a stalwart from the successful team of the 1990s and now a Man United ambassador to join my leaving do. He sat next to me at the table and told me various stories and anecdotes. It brings tears to my eyes that the Jewson gang knew me so well and invested in such an emotionally memorable event. An experience like that is so much more memorable than a gift or present—it is unique, incomparable and will always be treasured.

I then find myself walking past Old Trafford cricket stadium, which I have never seen before so a real sporting theme to my day. Cricket has always been a sport I have enjoyed watching albeit usually after football and rugby. I enjoyed watching Matthew and James play cricket for a couple of seasons—my abiding memory is the day that I nearly caused a fire engine to visit the cricket ground. Along with another dad I was on barbeque duty, cooking the burgers and sausages for hungry boys and parents watching the games outside the pavilion.

Unfortunately, the levels of fat had built up over time under the grill (in hindsight it had never been cleaned) and I am quite skilled at burning sausages usually through being distracted. A combination of the two factors resulted in the barbeque grease catching fire from the burning sausages and then suddenly the whole barbeque was in flames. We managed to use the fire extinguishers and put the fire out, but the sausages were covered in foam. I thought about passing it off as mayonnaise but was advised against it. The kids filled up on crisps, and I was never allowed on the barbeque there again.

I am delighted with the bed and breakfast at Prestbury. Thanks to Judith for kindly donating bed and breakfast at the White House Manor—a fantastic place, with a lovely room. I am staying tomorrow as well for my scheduled rest day. Further excitement for me when I discover that each room has a DVD player along with among others, James Bond DVDs for my rest day activity. Prestbury village is very picturesque with several nice eating places and a lovely coffee shop.

The owners inform me of a village club where they show football, and the Man Utd v Chelsea game could be on. It is! I am first in the hall and have several pints of Guinness (the match itself was a dull 0-0 but it is simply great to be here) which are delicious. Guinness is one of my favourite drinks although it does not reach the level of creaminess and taste of Irish Guinness. Andrew thinks that I go to Dublin frequently to visit him and the family but really, he is very much a sideshow to the Guinness.

While on the topic of Guinness—I also happen to hold (or maybe now it is past tense—held) two Guinness world records and not many people can say that. It is not for my speed in running, although I once came third out of about ten in a school 100-metre race (Usain is not really under threat), nor extreme strength. The first world record was achieved along with around 1200 others when at a Jewson customer event we had 'the most people wearing a Christmas jumper in one room simultaneously', impressive huh? The following year I/we obtained a second world record having the most people in one room wrapping a Christmas present at the same time and within a certain time limit.

In both cases, we had the Guinness officials attending to validate the claims as genuine. This makes a great ice breaker conversation. Back to the village hall and the other football followers who turn up are very generous and many contribute to my collection tin that I take with me wherever I go. The village hall owner told me that I could go and walk around the tables to collect money, it felt a bit intrusive, but I developed a good technique of explaining my story and asking whether they had any spare coppers—the outcome was more notes than coins.

News Headlines Context, 24 October 2020

In news headlines, Brexit breakthrough as trade talks could enter a crucial new phase next week. BREXIT negotiations could go into a crucial 'tunnel' phase as early as Monday as a trade deal looks to be within reach. Brexit deal could be reached if THREE key stumbling blocks are overcome this weekend— The first stumbling block to a free trade agreement is the issue of fishing rights. The second issue, which could sink a deal is the so-called 'level playing field' demand put forward by the Europeans.

The EU has called for commitments from the British to uphold its standards on labour rights, tax, subsidy law and the environment. And the other biggest issue blighting prospects of a deal is governance. Queen's staff spend a lot of time changing clocks at royal residences—Royal Collection Trust staff will spend more than 40 hours adjusting clocks at the Queen's official residences.

This includes 600 timepieces at Buckingham Palace, 450 at Windsor Castle and 50 at the Palace of Holyroodhouse.

Me: This is highly amusing—I have 3 clocks to change at home—I do not even wear a watch now as I use my mobile phone. I change my alarm clock, the clocks in the hall and lounge, which I can do without any help—and then the oven clock that I can never remember how to do it—so the 'support team' is always needed. Total of four minutes all in!

Coronavirus Daily Context, 24 October 2020

"Boris Johnson told Christmas lockdown will be rejected for 'creating more harm than good'. Bans on visiting relatives at Christmas will simply be ignored by the British public, ministers fear. A senior source said that the government believes it has 'reached the limit' with lockdowns and 'will need to ease restrictions over Christmas'. They suggested that discussions in Boris Johnson's top team have come to the conclusion that 'there cannot be a third lockdown' and while 'more areas will go into tier 3 [restrictions]' in the short term, the government is going to need to start easing them. They said: 'It is going to be very hard to expect people to not see their relatives at Christmas, and there is a real risk people will not follow the rules'."

Tracking new cases 16,235; deaths 213
(Source: coronavirus.data.gov.uk)

It is very tricky to get the balance of safety versus mental anguish over the Christmas period. We plan to have my parents over for the holiday period but there is no doubt that more people travelling, and mixing will fuel further cases—so it is a trade-off. In simple terms, I would prefer to take the pain of a harsher lockdown now in order to have a few days at Christmas with mum and dad.

Halloween prep in Salford.

Tram in Broadway.

Trafford Park.

Sir Alex Ferguson Way.

Theatre of Dreams.

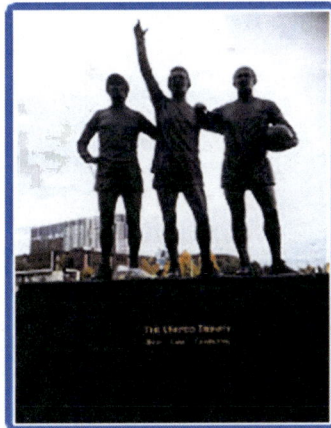

Law, Best, Charlton.

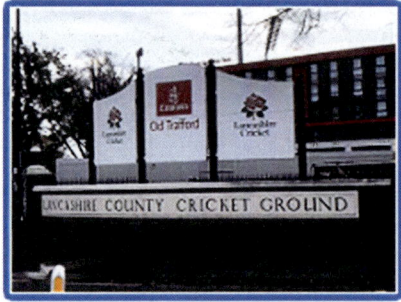

Old Trafford cricket stadium.

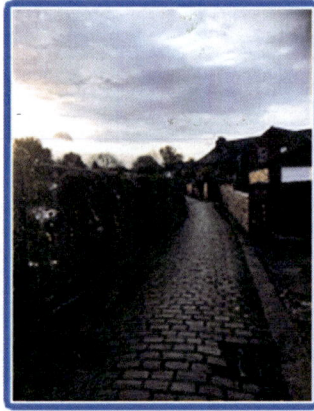

Chorlton (Coronation street esque)

Day 42. Sunday 25 October, Rest Day

Lovely high street Prestbury.

Rest day.

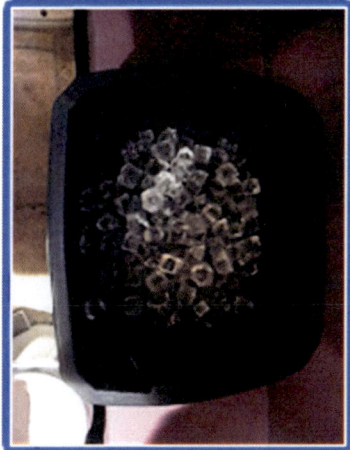

Great day off! (ice bucket for feet!)

Four Days Before Arriving at Milestone Four

Day 43. Monday 26 October, Prestbury to Newcastle Under Lyme

I am fully rested and ready for a typical autumnal walk—wind, showers, and sunshine. Mind you I have to set off twice today and walk an unnecessary extra half mile. I have no idea what made me think of it but having set off and completed a quarter of a mile I realise that I have left two of my walking shirts drying on the radiator. The shirts are white, and I have left them on a white radiator so did not notice when I was leaving the room.

I turn back, collect them, and set off again. It makes me think what distance would I have had to walk before I would have written them off? I think probably three quarters of a mile because that would have added 1 and a half miles to my total and an extra thirty mins. This is not a disaster though. Today is the first time my footpath has been blocked by a giant hedge trimmer as you will see in the photos below and this part of the world has some exceptionally large moles judging by the size of the divots that I come across.

My thoughts turn to what I will do after the walk is finished. Unless a job offer comes incredibly quickly then I still have the opportunity to use the time given to me constructively. I have always wanted to write a book so perhaps this can be the other output from the opportunity given to me. Over the years, I have wanted to write a variety of different book types, although I am not convinced that I am a natural author.

I love to read and always appreciate great fiction—Lee Child and John Grisham books always figure high on my list. I have a great sharing scheme with Dad who reads a lot—he shares them with me and then I share them with the boys or return them. In my mind, I could write a fiction novel or a book on leadership from a layman's point of view to combine it with personal examples and anecdotes.

I have only been in mainstream print once when many people will have read my contribution. As a child, I wrote to Whizzer and Chips (children's comic) and sent in a joke that I made up myself to earn myself the reward of £1. I can even remember it today, and it could equally well go into a Christmas cracker.

Q: What kind of cakes don't people like?

A: Stum-a-cakes (Stomach aches)

I am tempted to write a book and be able to knock it off my list—whether it is successful or not. Perhaps the best subject I could write about would be to turn this walk into a book and see if I can raise additional funds for the two charities.

Great support from the team at the Bull pub where I stop for coffee and soup—the manager donates lunch to the cause and the waitress donates to my trusty collection tin. I walk 23 miles today so one of my longer walks. Tonight, I am staying at the Borough Arms hotel in Newcastle under Lyme where I have a discounted room and breakfast and the manager kindly donates a cheque to me in a small ceremony in the bar where we look like a couple of 'Dick Turpins'.

News Headlines Context, 26 October 2020

In news headlines, NASA has announced the 'unambiguous' presence of water on the Moon. The discovery of water on the Moon is believed to be a significant boost for planned missions to the Moon, Mars and even beyond. Paul Hayne, assistant professor in the laboratory of atmospheric and space physics at the University of Colorado Boulder, said in a statement: 'Water is going to be more accessible for drinking water, for rocket fuel, everything that NASA needs water for'. UNITED States officials are mobilising their coastguard fleets following illegal fishing and harassment of vessels in the Pacific by China. The US national security adviser Robert O'Brien said new-generation Coast Guard vessels would conduct maritime security missions, such as fisheries patrols.

Me: So it is not just Britain versus Europe on fisheries—it is clearly a highly emotive topic—be good if we could all come together to manage the stocks and ensure quality stocks are available for future generations.

Coronavirus vaccine breakthrough: UK hospital on alert for deliveries next week. Health officials in London are on standby to take delivery of a new coronavirus vaccine from next week. A major hospital trust in London has been informed they should prepare to receive the first batches of the Oxford Astra-Zeneca vaccine from the 'week commencing the 2 November'.

Frontline doctors and nurses will be vaccinated at the hospital as soon as the Government gives the green light. There are security fears over potential anti-vaccination protests and so the hospital is planning to organise extra security measures. The UK's National Health Department last night said: 'The NHS has a tried and tested track record for delivering vaccination programmes'.

"We will work with existing partners across the healthcare system to ensure a COVID-19 vaccine can be deployed safely and effectively. 'A COVID-19 vaccine will only be deployed once it has been proven to be safe and effective through robust clinical trials'. It will have to be approved for use by the independent regulator."

Tracking new cases 26,555; deaths 277

(Source: coronavirus.data.gov.uk)

Positive talk seems to be accelerating on the vaccines, which is surely the only way through this. I do not take the flu jab as I have generally avoided catching that, but I do not see that as an option this time—I would prefer the Oxford vaccine once approved as it is a viral vector, not an mRNA vaccine.

Prestbury.

River Bollin.

Colourful flowers in Gawsworth.

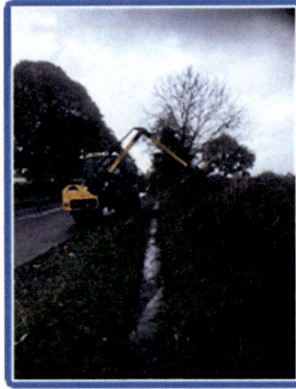

Blocked by hedge trimmer in Eaton.

River Dane.

Astbury Mere Country Park.

Giant moles in Brownlow.

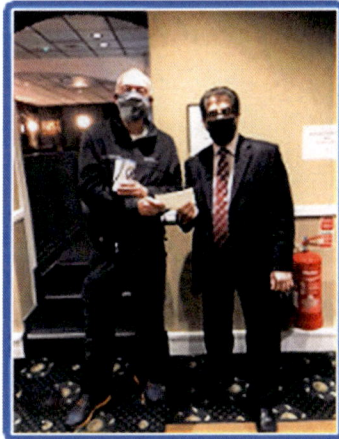

Cheque ceremony at Borough Arms Hotel.

Three Days Before Arriving at Milestone Four

Day 44. Tuesday 27 October, Newcastle Under Lyme to Newport, Telford

Today is generally a pleasant walk as I navigate the quieter and increasingly leafy lanes. I appreciate the regular phone calls from Andrew as it's generally a boost (not always) but particularly on the damper days such as today.

I am particularly close to both my brothers—Tim is three years younger than me, and Andrew is three years younger than Tim. I think the age gap is minimal particularly as you get older (although as children there are distinct advantages to staying up later as the younger siblings straggle reluctantly off to bed) and I think our closeness is a by-product of the close family ties that Mum and Dad have created. We visit each other regularly and whatever gap in time there is between visits, we all fall back into our regular roles.

I am not sure what bonds us. We have similar values and principles based on the way we have been brought up, and I think the sense of humour is a key contributor. The bond has only strengthened as we have got older, and between us and our respective nephews and nieces.

I like to think of myself as witty and able to amuse others with my banter— all three of us do—whether the comments are actually amusing is of course very subjective. Talking to Tim, I often inform him that I play to my strengths, which is to bring a smile to the faces of those that I am talking to, whereas his view is that I bring more of a grimace. I amuse myself, particularly, when others do not want to smile but I end up forcing them to against their will.

As children, when either Tim or Andrew was in a bad mood, I would tell them 'here comes a smile' in an annoying voice—but it would inevitably make them smile. In more recent times, I adopted a similar approach with James when he broke his nose playing rugby. His nose and face were very sore, and it hurt him to smile or laugh. Unfortunately, I could not resist pulling a face or cracking some funny comments that drew out the reluctant smile, and his trying to resist made me smile—and so the cycle went on.

Andrew and I have a similar approach to talking in silly voices sometimes—it probably originated in talking to our children when they were younger, but somehow this is often applied to all family members. We all enjoy staying with each other. I have been fortunate enough to stay over in London in recent years when Andrew has been over on work. We were able to plan our schedules and ensure a few pints in the pub along with a meal out.

When Andrew and Hilary moved over to Dublin a few years ago I took a week off work and helped him move the cars and some of their gear via ferry. It became a boys' tour with an overnight in Chester followed by a few days getting the home ready for Hilary and the children to come over. We definitely got the good end of the deal though—setting up furniture and visiting the local pubs/restaurants while Hilary, her sister and mother transported a 3-year-old and a 2-month-old across in an aeroplane.

Having taken 21-month-old twins to Australia on a plane many years ago (well actually before I am corrected by the 'support team', Anne took them out, and I only had to deal with the return journey) then I know some of the pitfalls. As we set up their new home ready for the family, and as my DIY skills are not one of my strengths, I was given the basic tasks (making tea) or I was closely supervised where I had to follow orders rather than building complicated furniture.

Another illustration of my poor practical skills occurred when we built new beds a few years ago from Ikea for Matthew and James—the results were not as they should have been. Anne helped Matthew whilst I 'helped' James. It is fair to say we were two quite different teams. Anne and Matthew both are practical, have an eye for design and can translate from an instruction leaflet to reality.

James and I cannot. Anne and Matthew completed their bed very quickly. James and I did not. Matthew's bed execution is exactly as it should be according to the picture. James has one drawer bottom upside down and all 4 drawers sticking out beyond the mattress frame. But James and I did at least laugh a lot as we built it and that is the value I bring.

But back to my brothers. When I was working in the Midlands, I would plan a night away whenever I could stay with Tim and Elaine rather than overnight in a hotel. This enabled us to have some quality banter (although I am not sure all would have a common definition of the term) and a catch-up—usually watching a blockbuster film as well. One time, I recall Matthew and I stayed with Tim, as Matthew was checking out Birmingham University as one of his options. We had a Chinese takeaway—I can still see the white/grey fish head on one of the dishes even today. At the time, the food was lovely but the following day I was retching. Nobody else was ill, and I put it down to the fish head. I ended up managing to drive Matthew to the university and then crashing out on the back seat of the car in the car park with a plastic bag into which I continued to retch, while Matthew went around the university on his own. Lovely memories.

I am staying in the Premier Inn tonight as I could not find a local B&B. The big positive when staying in Premier Inn is the bed—it's large and wonderfully comfortable, and they always are—great brand consistency. I realise that at the end of each day the shower is what I really look forwards to—it washes away the aches, pains and rain residue, I even do my stretching in there when the space allows. Although as a friend posted on Facebook 'that's too much detail, David'.

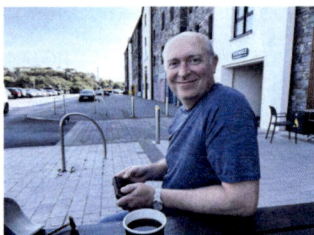

Andrew. Some more rain today, so some more fun with calls to both phones to ensure the maximization of pocket rummaging in the rain. However, the biggest recollection for this day was the lack of planning around dinner whilst at the Premier Inn; I think there was a visit to a local shop for an odd assortment of pork pies (acceptable) but also things like mini quiches (odd).

News Headlines Context, 27 October 2020

In news headlines, One lucky UK ticket-holder has won today's £79 million EuroMillions jackpot, the National Lottery has revealed. China sets sights on Antarctica grab as coronavirus fuels 'no diplomacy' in the Southern Ocean. Experts now fear Beijing is looking south, to the scientific haven of Antarctica, hoping to position itself as a global leader in the region and push its luck with an international treaty. The global pact, signed 60 years ago, is dedicated to preserving and protecting the continent for scientific research and provides a safeguard against nuclear proliferation.

Coronavirus Daily Context, 27 October 2020

"In news headlines, death rates for 'COVID' hospitalised patients half first wave. Death rates of people hospitalised with coronavirus have halved since the peak of the first wave of the pandemic earlier this year, breakthrough new research has revealed. Two million more people could face Tier 3—council bosses in emergency talks. Around two million more people in the north of England could be placed under the toughest coronavirus restrictions after councils warned further measures are needed to curb the spread of COVID-19. Local officials in West Yorkshire have held emergency talks with senior ministers and Deputy Chief Medical Officer Professor Jonathan Van-Tam over the rise of infections and hospital admissions in the region. Around 1.8 million people in Leeds, Kirklees, Calderdale, Bradford and Wakefield are currently living under Tier 2 restrictions—with curbs placed on households mixing."
Tracking new cases 24,105; deaths 266
(Source: coronavirus.data.gov.uk)

Other than Colne where I escaped with 24 hours' notice and Salford where I was unable to stay with Julie as planned, I have been incredibly lucky to stay ahead of the local lockdown ground rules. It feels like I am slightly ahead of an avalanche with balls of ice growing and gaining momentum—snapping at my heels as I slalom down the black run in my skis…. which is kind of ironic as I can barely parallel ski on a blue run.

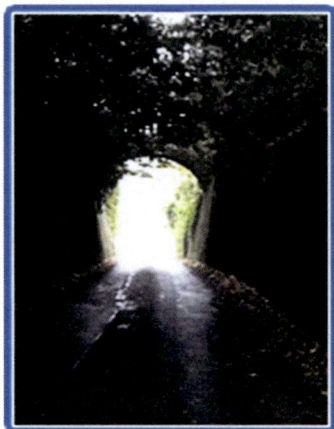

'Light at the end of the tunnel'.

Maer Hall Bromley Pool.

Fair Oak.

Two Days Before Arriving at Milestone Four

Day 45. Wednesday 28 October, Newport, Telford to Wolverhampton

The first mile today on the main A road is horrible but as soon as I find the smaller lanes again it improves greatly and there is hardly any traffic. The sun comes out, and I notice that my average walking speed is holding up nicely—it's typically 3.2–3.4 mph versus my first week walking (also known as 'blistergate') where I was often under 3 mph. I am also faster in the morning sessions than in the afternoons. The presence of the sun makes such a difference to the quality of the photos—when the sun is out it brings a rich vibrancy to the deep red, green and blue colours. One of the photos that I take in Shackerley is more of a pastel watercolour and reminds me of a Monet type painting. I spot a Costa coffee shop and find a seat before a double whammy of the heavens opening and the school mums and kids bundling inside, resulting in the remaining seats being taken. The Costa manager kindly donates the latte, and I manage to get online and work through my emails. I need to investigate if a toasted teacake counts as one of my five a day.

It's great at this stage when all my accommodation is lined up so unless something changes, I do not need to focus on that. I walk past my second big stadium today—the mighty Wolves. I have not been here before, and it looks impressive.

Perhaps that could be a future walk to visit all the football stadiums and sample the pie and a pint experience (post-COVID of course). Tonight, I am staying at the Britannia in Wolverhampton—many thanks for donating the room and continental breakfast.

News Headlines Context, 28 October 2020

In news headlines, hopes of a Brexit deal were handed a boost after British and European Union negotiators edged closer to a compromise. The two sides were said to be close to finalising a draft legal text on future common standards, including state subsidies for businesses, as part of a tentative breakthrough in the talks. Lord Frost and EU counterpart Michel Barnier are expected to pass the negotiations up to Boris Johnson and European Commission chief Ursula von der Leyen to take a decision on the final trade-offs.

In France, President Macron introduces a second nationwide France lockdown with permission needed to leave home. The French President used a televised address to announce another sweeping lockdown to combat France's spiralling coronavirus cases. France recorded 33,417 new cases, as well as 523 new deaths, yesterday. It comes as Mr Macron is facing a wave of unrest from the French, with anti-lockdown protests sweeping across Europe.

Coronavirus Daily Context, 28 October 2020

We have to start seeing COVID deaths in their true (tiny) context or it will ruin Britain. IT'S GREAT news that older volunteers are responding positively to a COVID-19 vaccine developed at Oxford University Blood tests on over-55s reveal that the release of antibodies provides a robust defence against the disease. Because if there is anything this country needs to battle the economic catastrophe wrought by the pandemic it is the confidence to return back to normal life and an early vaccine guarantees that. It is older generations that are most vulnerable to coronavirus, and it is they who must be at the front of the queue for the vaccine. It is a 'key milestone', says Oxford University, and is part of a clinical trial testing thousands of volunteers across several countries.

"The sooner this data is passed to regulators the sooner it can be rolled out across the UK. Already improved methods of dealing with coronavirus have meant that doctors and nurses are more adept at saving lives, so the second spike in cases this autumn need not be as lethal as the first wave was in the spring. The UK has recorded 367 more COVID-19 deaths in the latest 24-hour period—the darkest day since the end of May—but the outbreak is continuing to slow with another 22,885 infections, a rise of just 7% in a week. The average age of those

lives tragically cut short is 82.4 years old. Virtually all young people have
nothing to fear from catching the disease."

   Tracking new cases 23,616; deaths 283
   (Source: coronavirus.data.gov.uk)

I am not sure if I fall into the 'older generation' or 'young people' definition regarding the 'at-risk' definition. No, I have decided—I am in the 'young people' group.

Sunrise.

Aqualate 'Monet' type photo.

Shackerley Wolverhampton football stadium.

Day Before Arrival at Milestone Four

Day 46. Thursday 29 October, Wolverhampton to Kidderminster

I must admit that Wolverhampton does not appeal to me compared to some of the other locations I have stayed in, with regard to scenery/character, and I am not expecting much on the walk to Kidderminster but once I get off the main road there are some lovely lanes and villages. The photos do not really do the scenes justice as it is a little damp.

One of my many pleasures from the walk has been the regular supportive calls I get from Andrew. He phones me three times a day, every day, and it's great just to talk, and listen to, nonsense, which we both excel at. It is probably an amusing sight when he calls, particularly if it is raining. It takes me a few minutes to untangle the wires and remove the protective plastic bag.

By which time, I have missed the call. Then I hear my other phone ringing, and I repeat the procedure only this time, if I can answer, then I can no longer see the map to follow the route. One day I recall having to retrace my steps for half a mile as I missed the turning due to talking nonsense. I enjoy the scenery around Enville—it is just me and 'Mother Nature' together and the rich blend of reds, browns, and greens in the context of woods or forest remind me of Centre Parcs.

> Andrew: I remember speaking to David whilst it was raining. I knew it was raining as he did not answer either phone which usually means rain, or he is already on a call, or he is lost and needing to find his location. Whichever scenario it is that is barring me from speaking, brings a devilish joy in calling the other phone just to make sure he has heard it, and probably annoyed by it.

CentreParcs deliver a great experience that is consistent across all their locations and the accommodation is very cleverly designed to fit in with the wooded surroundings and maintain privacy. We have been going as a full family for many years—kindly funded by the bank of mum and dad—and it is an annual chance to get Tim, Andrew, Mum and Dad, me and our families together usually sharing two adjoining lodges. When the children were younger, we would hire their bicycles and in more recent years it evolved into a trip to the pub area to watch a big football or rugby match and have a few beers.

There are a couple of constants whatever the ages of the children—trips to the swimming pool and at least one barbeque held outdoors (often cooking under umbrellas). I love the swimming pool and more specifically the rapids and the slides. I am undoubtedly the most excitable adult, and, in many ways, the next generation are more mature than me; it is not usually me that says we have been on the slides long enough and we now need to leave.

The rapids are particularly amusing as we gather as many of us as possible (usually Tim, Andrew, me, and our respective children) at the top of the rapids and then aim to barge each other into the sidewalls of the rapids to be crushed or alternatively to get beached at the side. Sticking big toes into each other's faces is also highly amusing. With Aoife and Edward only four and two years old respectively, they are not quite ready for the 'Rapids challenge' but it will come.

I also entertain myself in the evenings by planting solid awkwardly shaped objects under the bed sheets or pillowcases in my brothers' rooms designed to cause maximum irritation at bedtime. Unfortunately, the next generation learns quickly, and I am now more often the victim rather than the perpetrator. Anyway, Centre Parcs is an annual highlight (pre-COVID) for me.

I walk a solid 18 miles today, and I realise that one week today, all being well, I will cross the finish line. Today is also my final day for a few days with the big rucksack as my parents have kindly offered to collect it from my accommodation in Kidderminster tomorrow and take it to their house where I am staying. I stop for coffee and teacake in Kinver, which proves to be a lovely large village and the staff kindly donate their tips into the collection tin. Thanks also to Gainsborough House where I am staying in Kidderminster and which kindly donates a bed to the cause.

News Headlines Context, 29 October 2020

In news headlines, Jeremy Corbyn has been suspended from Labour after he accused the party's anti-Semitism problem of being 'overstated'. A spokesperson for the Labour Party said: 'In light of his comments made today and his failure to retract them subsequently, the Labour Party has suspended Jeremy Corbyn pending investigation. He has also had the whip removed from the Parliamentary Labour Party'. But Mr Corbyn hit back at Labour's decision, and tweeted: 'I will strongly contest the political intervention to suspend me'. In Paris, armed police have swarmed to Champs-Elysees on suspicion of a bomb threat in Paris—it comes as France remains on high alert after an earlier attack in Nice today and a beheading northwest of the capital earlier this month.

Coronavirus Daily Context, 29 October 2020

"In news headlines, holiday devastation as new European hotspots axed from travel corridors. Cyprus holidays now face ruin following the latest travel corridor change. The announcement that both Cyprus and Lithuania would lose their travel corridor and face quarantine restrictions was announced on Thursday evening. Coronavirus news: The 'R' rate rising near 'three in

London'—UK hotspots revealed. Coronavirus continues to dominate lives—tighter restrictions are in force throughout the United Kingdom; now the 'R' rate is creeping up to 'three' in London—the UK hotspots revealed. In order for the pandemic to slow down, and reduce in numbers, the 'R' number needs to be below one. Across England, the 'R' rate (the rate of reproduction) is estimated to be 1.6. The report summarised its findings: 'The epidemic is now increasing most rapidly in the Midlands and South.' Patterns of growth rate and the age distribution of cases in the South now are similar to those observed in northern regions during the prior two rounds of this study."

Tracking new cases 23,345; deaths 309

(Source: coronavirus.data.gov.uk)

The rate of acceleration on infections and deaths continues—we are now at over 300 deaths per day. The North of the country has clearly been impacted recently, and it looks like Midlands and the South will be impacted next. Once again, I am slightly ahead or in line with the virus trend.

Cookley.

Broadwaters Park.

Arriving at Gainsborough House Hotel.

Halloween approaching.

Day of Arrival at Milestone Four

Day 47. Friday 30 October, Kidderminster to Milestone 4

I set off early and pass a very aptly named pub—'The Weary Traveller'—and a very smart new fire station for Hereford & Worcester. A fantastic day in so many ways—and I am so excited to meet my parents later, I am 'rucksack less' if there is such a phrase, I am completing leg four of the five, and I find a route to walk along the towpath—the Severn Way, for several miles. I only see one person in over seven miles. There is only one problem this morning.

As I do not have a rucksack today, I have two bottles of water, which I store in my left- and right-hand side jacket pockets. I find a nice tree for my mid-morning toilet break, and unfortunately, both bottles of water fell out of my pockets and onto the ground. The luck is not with me as one of the bottles lands with the lid touching some residue dog waste, previously invisible due to the number of leaves. I am fortunate, I guess, that the other bottle was OK, as along the river Severn there are not many coffee shops or convenience stores to replenish.

Also, for some reason, the Strava app does not work properly today, and it does not capture the miles I walk along the towpath. I see another potential business idea if my Dave's cafe idea does not work out—then Dave's Gardening services could be a fallback. I walk 20 miles though and am now at 530—tantalisingly close to my 616-mile target. It was so nice not having the rucksack today. It is not the weight or the stress on the back that is uncomfortable I think it is just putting extra pressure on my feet.

Overall, my feet are holding up well though. The big right toe area is a bit sore, and they are still gammon like in their appearance but so far there are no new blisters since I returned to the walk. I have come to appreciate the tortoise and turtle who carry all their possessions, including their homes, on their backs—in reality, nature has designed them for this capability, and I was not built with an integrated rucksack compartment attached to my back.

In 1980, there was a big upheaval as we moved to a new house again due to Dad's promotion at work. Not just a small move from one part of town to the other—more like one side of the country to the other. The house though that we moved to was fantastic. Located on the side of the hills with a nice front lawn and two-tiered back lawn with space for swings and a mini football pitch/badminton court. Tim and Andrew were also desperate for a pet, so we ended up with a Golden Labrador as part of the deal.

Mum and Dad collect me after my 20-mile walk and drop me at my old school—**The Chase High School in Great Malvern**—which is the first visit for milestone four. The school has not changed at all, and it is strange going back after so many years. This is where I progressed from my early years as an inept footballer and developed my Paul Scholes midfield general skills—it was just unfortunate that the scouts from the big football clubs never picked the right games to observe me. I enjoy seeing our old house again, we were so lucky to live halfway up the hills with easy access walking to the Beacon and the British Camp as well as the local common where we would walk our dog. We then drive up to the front of the house in College Grove, Great Malvern and which has been renovated recently. I notice the walls in the front garden are still standing despite my DIY efforts many years ago. I had been asked by Dad to help repair the walls as many of the stones were coming loose—I blended the mixture components with water and refixed the loose stones, all seemed well until it was noted the following day that I had forgotten to add the cement mixture and the stones were still loose. I still claimed my pocket money though and added to my expanding reputation for poor practical skills.

Malvern just had to be milestone four—mum and dad still live here, and we spent more your years living in the house in College Grove than any other.

It is great to spend tonight and tomorrow's rest day with mum and dad. We are incredibly lucky to have such special parents, I guess most families think the same, but they really are the figureheads of the Fenton family. In discussion with friends and colleagues, it would appear, there are not many families where several generations enjoy spending time together on holiday. Friends of ours often do not go on holiday with their kids as their interests are so different yet we meet up across three generations every year.

Mum and Dad laid out their values early on and we are the by-product of nature combined with nurture. I would sum up the family moral code as trying to do what's right at the right time. I remember once as a youngster being cheeky back to my parents when I asked them to be quiet as I was trying to watch children's TV. My logic was that I had to be quiet when they were viewing the evening news. I was subsequently sent to my room for being cheeky, although I discovered a technique where I could lie at the top of the stairs discreetly and watch TV from afar without being spotted.

I also recall some stressful mealtimes as children. Tim is the sensible one and usually made it unscathed through mealtimes. I would often get the giggles and be sent away from the meal either to my bedroom or to the outhouse until I could stop giggling. Andrew, knowing this, would often instigate something to start me giggling—but he did not think ahead and realise that would then start him giggling also, thus he would be sent from the mealtime along with me—but sent to a different location.

I am not quite sure in hindsight how the relationship between parents and children evolves to one that is more of equals than hierarchical. Maybe it just happens naturally, but since we became teenagers, it seemed natural to be 'respectfully cheeky' with mum and dad, and I am sure we got away with more—certainly, the boys do with Anne and me. Mum and Dad are always there for us and always supportive.

Somehow, they always find the right things to say at the right time. They were great with Matthew and James when the boys were young—mum would often come to visit to help Anne out with the babies when I was away with work and dad would often comfort James when he would wake up crying with colic. I realise as well that playing card games with mum and dad, watching a family film, having a nice holiday—which we effectively replicate now with our boys—has become part of the Fenton culture, so we have been fortunate indeed to have such loving, caring parents raise us.

After my shower, it is straight into tea and lemon cake followed quickly by gin and tonic for a change, and pork scratchings specially purchased as a treat. Mum inspects my feet as they are being iced, and I pass her scrutiny—phew!

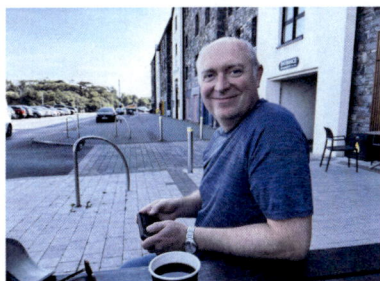

Andrew: A great joy talking through where he was at particular points in the day (for me anyway). I always have a fondness for Malvern; we all do. We all went to the same school, although obviously David was a long time before I went (it might even have been coal powered back then). A nice by-product of the calls were the stories that were provoked and the emotions that came with them. It was also nice knowing he was spending some time with the parents - they would like that almost as much as he did!

Mum and Dad: It was great for us that David organized a "rest day" in Malvern and stayed two nights, even if it involved going out to buy a washing up bowl (didn't fancy using ours!) and Epsom Salts. Also filled the freezer with ice cubes. We were going to present him with the bowl and remaining Epsom Salts all wrapped up for Christmas but, alas, a family get together abandoned due to COVID.

News Headlines Context, 30 October 2020

In news headlines, Ryanair has suspended all flights from regional Irish airports for a month, pointing the finger of blame at 'government mismanagement'. The news comes amid stringent travel and lockdown restrictions in the nation. India has destroyed a ship in the Bay of Bengal in a massive show of force by the state amid escalating tensions with China. The Indian Navy fired an anti-ship missile as military forces conducted naval drills in the region today.

Coronavirus Daily Context, 30 October 2020

"While cases remain highest in the north of England, a dramatic increase in infections has been recorded across all areas, according to the latest interim findings from the React-1 study from Imperial College London. The results triggered warnings from scientists that current measures, including bans on

households mixing and bars and pubs closed, are not working, and that urgent action is needed to avoid a sharp rise in hospital admissions and deaths. The React-1 study found that infections are still highest among 18–24-year-olds (2.2%) but are spreading into older and more vulnerable age groups. The percentage of people infected aged 55-64 increased more than three times from 0.37% to 1.2%. In the south-west, which had a low prevalence of infections, there I now a rise in infections among 18-24-year-olds. Professor Paul Elliott, director of the program, said: 'We're seeing a pattern in the south, which is similar to what we saw in the north a few weeks back'."

Tracking new cases 22,680; deaths 339

(Source: coronavirus.data.gov.uk)

When I look at the percentages impacted by the virus the numbers still seem low across the age groups, however, when you consider the total numbers of deaths and the impact on the hospitals then it is clearly significant. I didn't realise that Paul Elliot who once played for Chelsea as a centre back, is now a professor and leading figure in the fight against the virus.

Pertinent: The Weary Traveller.

Kidderminster New fire station.

Kidderminster River.

Stour Astley.

Barge at Ombersley.

Dave's gardening services—Worcester.

View of the Malvern Hills.

The Chase High School Malvern.

Arriving at the Chase.

Arriving at College Grove.

Thanks, mum—Tea and lemon cake.

Day 48. Saturday 31 October—Rest Day

I do not normally write an update on a rest day but the announcement from Boris Johnson concerning the next lockdown timing and logistics is delayed by an hour and a half tonight impacting the international rugby game between Italy and England and nearly impacting Strictly Come Dancing (although amusingly the BBC refused to delay the start time for this).

I apologise to all those affected by the delay but it took me a while to get through and explain to Boris and his advisers that my walk finishes on Thursday so could they please build this into their planning when scheduling the next national lockdown. Fortunately, they were very receptive, it was all agreed, and the new lockdown is scheduled to kick in from Thursday, which is the day I plan to finish. Perfect.

Four Days Before Arriving at Milestone Five

Day 49. Sunday 1 November, Malvern to Tewkesbury

I am extremely excited to enter the final week and am fully refreshed after being spoiled by my parents and having watched three games of rugby to conclude the six nations championship with my feet permanently elevated. Today is a very gentle 12 miles, and I am looking forward to staying at the Tewkesbury Park hotel where the owners have kindly donated bed and breakfast—from the website it looks lovely. It is a nice walk to Upton on Severn, and I attempt to find coffee, but nothing is open at 9:00 a.m. on a Sunday morning.

My walking shoes are well and truly worn in now, and I continue walking along the Severn Way, which is great. As well as the scenic views and peace and quiet, I do not have to worry about other pedestrians or cars when needing a comfort break. I arrive early afternoon in Tewkesbury, which I have not visited in years, and I have forgotten what a lovely town it is. I find a large Costa with plenty of space to dump all my gear and enjoy a latte.

Tomorrow, I will have the large rucksack back on, as my parents drop it off later today, so I enjoy the freedom while I can. Tewkesbury Park is one of my favourite stays—a lovely hotel and a fantastic room. It is a shame Anne is not here tonight, as she would have appreciated the spa facilities and the food. The hotel works on the extra touches to give a great customer experience. The room is nice and warm, there is a 'well done' on the achievement postcard that is positioned on the bed for me when I enter the room, and the hotel has laid out a plate of fresh fruit.

Absolutely fantastic. Furthermore, I want to watch the football match, which is available in the leisure centre, however, they are due to close at 5:00 p.m. and the game kicks off at 5:30 p.m. A word or two with the team on duty, and they arrange to "lock me in" with a couple of beers (and a treat packet of pork scratchings donated by dad). The only thing they cannot arrange is the result and Man Utd lose 1-0 to Arsenal.

News Headlines Context, 1 November 2020

In news headlines, Donald Trump has overtaken Joe Biden in a vital poll, raising alarm bells for the Democratic hopeful. According to a poll by Des Moines Register and the Mediacom Iowa Poll, the Republican President has overtaken his presidential rival in Iowa. Mr Trump now leads by seven percentage points over Mr Biden, 48% to 41%. A Suspected Russian spy vessel has been discovered off the British coast close to the UK's Faslane nuclear submarine base amid fears Moscow has acquired the 'acoustic signature' of Britain's nuclear submarines.

The unmanned 'spy boat', powered by solar energy, is feared to be a part of Vladimir Putin's espionage programme. The autonomous vessel was found off the coast of Scotland last month, it has now been revealed, and was designed for stealth so as to avoid detection by UK-based surveillance sensors. Russia has yet to come forward to claim it as their own.

Coronavirus Daily Context, 1 November 2020

In news headlines, Boris handed blueprint to beat coronavirus without lockdown—doctors reveal masterplan. Boris Johnson has been handed a blueprint for defeating coronavirus, which does not involve the misery of another national lockdown. Professor Carl Heneghan, director at The Centre for Evidence-Based Medicine at the University of Oxford, and British epidemiologist Dr Tom Jefferson have outlined four key issues the Prime Minister must address to curb the spread of the virus. Professor Heneghan and Dr Jefferson base their strategy on two key principles, the first being a lockdown does not work in the long term and only serves to 'kick the can down the road'.

The second is to establish an end game to the virus, which does not do 'more damage than the virus itself'. In their four-point plan presented to Boris Johnson more than a month ago, they said the Government needs to make radical changes to how COVID-19 is recorded with NHS Test and Trace, present clear statistics to the public, protect vulnerable groups and explain the quantifiable costs of lockdowns. They argued if these four issues were solved then there would be 'real hope that we can learn to live with the virus'.

"Coronavirus chaos: the UK reports over 23k cases as England approaches critical lockdown. Coronavirus cases in England rose to 23,254 in the past 24 hours as the country heads into lockdown from Thursday."

Tracking new cases 15,751; deaths 358

(Source: coronavirus.data.gov.uk)

An interesting four-point plan that would avoid the need for a national lockdown, but I am not convinced they can all be resolved before the national lockdown starts in four days. It is all very well—and necessary—having key principles but if the advisers can help advise on 'how' to solve the four issues raised then I am sure that Boris would be highly appreciative.

Leaving Malvern.

Looking back at the Malverns.

Hanley Castle.

Upton Upon Severn.

Longdon Heath.

Tewkesbury Abbey.

Fruit awaiting.

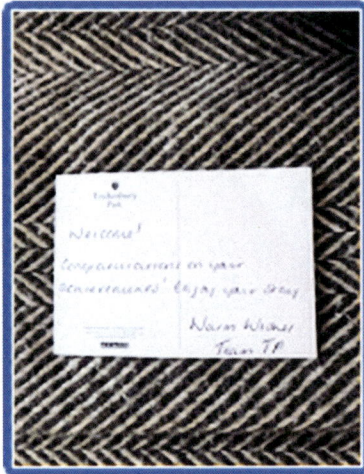

Lovely Congratulations Card.

Well-earned relaxation.

Three Days Before Arriving at Milestone Five

Day 50. Monday 2 November, Tewkesbury to Kineton

It is great to have the sun back with me today although not quite so nice to have the backpack on again after a couple of days without it. A lovely breakfast followed by a 'gentle' walk as it's only 17 miles today. I say gentle, and it is in terms of miles—the elevation felt quite high as I walked across the Cotswolds although the data on Strava did not support this. The sun really brings the autumnal colours to life so again I captured some lovely photos.

I am staying at the Halfway House in Kineton tonight, and I am incredibly grateful to Sarah who is donating bed and breakfast. Along with her husband and family, they have only been running the pub for eight weeks and are trying to adapt to the consequences of the virus as it impacts their business—focusing on providing a takeaway service to reduce the impact on their revenue. The location in Kineton is picturesque and my stay here is another of my favourites. I have a lovely room and am very well looked after—great beer and a very enjoyable combination of pate followed by fish and chips. The Cotswolds and Kineton/Guiting area, in particular, will be on my target list to revisit at a later date.

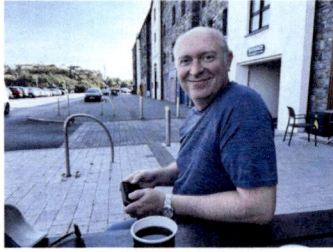

> Andrew: So, this was an interesting time for David. He had been looking forwards to the various goals, particularly when i) it was not raining and ii) when there was a pub to aim for at the end of the day. However, around this time, there was a dawning sense that the ultimate goal, the end of the road [if you will excuse the pun], was now rapidly approaching. I recall that the excitement of being reunited with The Support Team was strong, and in parallel the rest of normality was not as spine-tingling. Perhaps the journey does not end at 616 miles after all...?

News Headlines Context, 2 November 2020

In news headlines, Vienna terror attack: 'Hostages taken at restaurant' as police say six sites targeted. Hostages are being held in a restaurant in Vienna following a terror attack in the Austrian capital, the police said an attack in Vienna on Monday night involved six crime scenes. One person had been killed and several hurt, including a police officer. One perpetrator has been shot dead according to police.

Leech pulled 'wriggling' from boy's BODY after living as a parasite for 'over a year. The parasite was removed from the boy's throat after a lengthy operation in China's southwestern Yunnan Province. The young boy had been suffering from recurring symptoms such as a sore throat, breathing difficulties, and snoring. The leech measured 2.75 inches and was discovered by a Chinese ear, nose, and throat specialist called Doctor Zhu Weihong.

Coronavirus Daily Context, 2 November 2020

"COVID: Scientists report T-cell immunity in major boost—'Cautiously optimistic'. COVID UK: Coronavirus cases continue to rise across the country, as Boris Johnson announces a second nationwide lockdown to curb the spread of the infection. But scientists are 'cautiously optimistic' after a new study showed that patients may have a level of immunity from COVID-19 for at least six months after the onset of symptoms. Six million Britons over the age of 60 should now follow the same coronavirus precautions as the 'clinically vulnerable' after the age range was lowered from the first wave."

Tracking new cases 31,506; deaths 330
(Source: coronavirus.data.gov.uk)

It is a 'ying and yang' COVID update today—encouraging signs around the levels of immunity duration post-COVID, on the other hand, the definition of vulnerable has broadened to include those in their sixties.

Leaving Tewkesbury Park.

Tewkesbury Park.

251

Tewkesbury Park.

Tewkesbury Park.

Tewkesbury Park.

Tewkesbury Park.

Guiting Power.

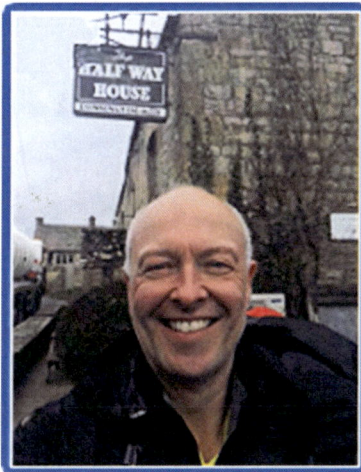

Arriving at Half Way House Kineton.

Two Days Before Arriving at Milestone Five

Day 51. Tuesday 3 November, Kineton to Shipton Under Wychwood

A lovely day walking from Kineton to Shipton under Wychwood and a rare occasion for me to recover and use my sunglasses—although it was raining again by the end of the day. Today is my final day with the rucksack as Anne is joining me later and will be able to transport it for me. Unbelievable though that by the end of the day I have developed 2 blisters—one on each foot and in the same place (fourth toe on each foot) where I had them previously. Yet I have not had any problem with blisters since the first week.

The only thing I can attribute it to is the heavy rucksack along with walking up hills, although I managed fine in the Yorkshire Dales. This is really frustrating for me as I have been so careful to manage my feet, I have iced them and elevated them and moisturised them. I am 3 days away from finishing and cannot believe I have to deal with the gammon steaks that now have a couple of poached eggs on the fourth toe on each foot, respectively. Whatever happens, my feet will not stop me—but I wanted to sprint across the finish line on Thursday not hire a Zimmer frame.

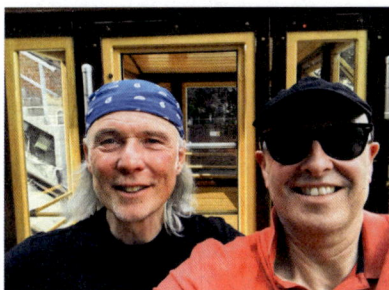

Jeremy. "Dave's John Rambo-like ability to 'ignore pain' was demonstrated to me a few years ago when he accompanied me on one of my annual ski sojourns to Zermatt. During our first day on the slopes, his rented ski boots were proving uncomfortable, to say the least, as they started to dig out gouges of flesh from his shins like the Swiss scrape away at the melted cheese block on a raclette grill! Nothing an ever-resourceful Dave couldn't overcome with a few Kleenex stuffed into his boots the next day, though!"

Some beautiful villages today notably Bourton-on–the-Water where I stop for refreshments. I walk 16 miles in total, and I am incredibly grateful to Abilio, the owner of the Shaven Crown who kindly donates bed and breakfast. The Shaven Crown is closed on Monday and Tuesday, but Abilio really goes above and beyond in his support for me. He opens the hotel so that Anne, and I are the only guests, he gives us a great spacious room, he contacts a nearby restaurant to let them know we were coming (and the restaurant then donates our dinner to the cause).

In addition, Abilio introduces us to Giles, the sales manager for Hook Norton Brewery speciality beers—Giles kindly donates bottles of beer and beer glasses that we can sell off to boost the funding. Anne, and I will return to the Shaven Crown and sign up for a visit to the nearby Hook Norton Brewery where you can book onto a tour and experience the sights, sounds, and smells of brewing beer the Hooky way. Apparently, you are guided around the 5-storey Victorian Tower Brewery and finish with a half-hour tasting of the handcrafted ales.

The Shaven Crown was founded in the fourteenth century by the monks of Bruern Abbey to house pilgrims and as a hospice for the poor and needy. Following the dissolution of the monasteries in the sixteenth century the Crown seized the hotel and Queen Elizabeth I later used it as a royal hunting lodge. Subsequently, it was given to the village on condition that it became an inn with the proceeds being used to help the poor.

Early in the twentieth century, the inn passed into private ownership and was named the Shaven Crown in homage to its founders. Through the centuries, it has maintained its charm, and many original features remain, including the fourteenth-century gateway and the double-braced roof structure of the iconic Great Hall.

(www.theshavencrown.co.uk/about)

Thanks to both Abilio and Giles. I am very conscious following numerous conversations with the pub and B&B owners where I have been staying, just what a hard time the industry is having, and this will be further exacerbated with the new national lockdown from Thursday. It makes their generosity even more overwhelming, and I would like to say "thank you" to everybody that has helped me or donated to the cause—and often both.

With a little persuasion, the support team posted a poll for me to the Facebook followers (over 160 of them). As I approach the end of the walk and look ahead to the weekend I want to 'ask the audience' how I should best fill my time. Option 1—put my feet up and get brought tea, coffee, beer depending on the time of day. Option 2—I am given a 'to-do' jobs list of all the things that have not been done over the last few weeks. Most of the Facebook followers voted for option 1 (phew) and the most amusing response was from my cousin who said option 1—but very quickly followed by option 2.

News Headlines Context, 3 November 2020

In news headlines, the furlough scheme is now being extended until December. The Government says the scheme will wind down when England comes out of lockdown. The Treasury has not provided an exact date, but the

Chancellor of the Exchequer tweeted that the scheme would run for 'another month'. Given that it was due to end on 31 October, this means the scheme would likely end on November 30. Riots broke out in Paris this morning, as high school students protested against the lack of social distancing in schools. Dozens of high school students were involved in the protests, which took place outside several Parisian schools. Violent scenes erupted outside Lycée Colbert, in the 10th arrondissement in Paris, as police attempted to disperse students by charging into them and spraying tear gas.

Coronavirus Daily Context, 3 November 2020

"In news headlines, coronavirus vaccine breakthrough as 'NHS to be put on standby for December rollout'. A coronavirus vaccine could be announced imminently and possibly rolled out on the front line as early as December. It is understood practices and Primary Care Network's (PCN's) will be able to start administering the potential vaccine to the front line from the beginning of December. PCN's are groups of practices working together to focus on local patient care. According to GP's magazine Pulse, practices and PCN's will be asked to give the potential vaccine to over-85s and front line workers as early as next month. There are currently two frontrunners in the development of a potential vaccine including Pfizer and Oxford/AstraZeneca."

Tracking new cases 25,591; deaths 362
(Source: coronavirus.data.gov.uk)

Now that is an encouraging virus update ahead of the imminent lockdown. It is a very strange feeling I have as I approach the conclusion of my walk. The fact is that the national lockdown starts the very day that my walk finishes. If I had missed one day through illness or my re-start had been one day later then I would not have been able to complete the walk.

The coronavirus whirlwind now has three elements—the tornado of deaths, which continues to go upwards rapidly, the unrelenting blizzard of national lockdown, which will start tomorrow, and the chink of sunlight glimpsed afar suggesting that the vaccine could be in effect from next month. I am forty-eight hours away from victory in the midst of all this.

Full English—lovely!

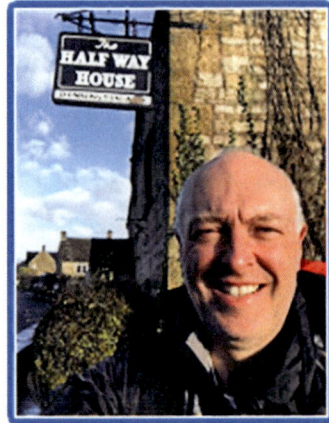

Leaving the Half Way House.

Guiting Power.

Naunton.

Upper Slaughter.

Bourton-on-the-Water.

Rainbow: Milton-under-Wychwood.

Many gnomes-Shipton-under-Wychwood.

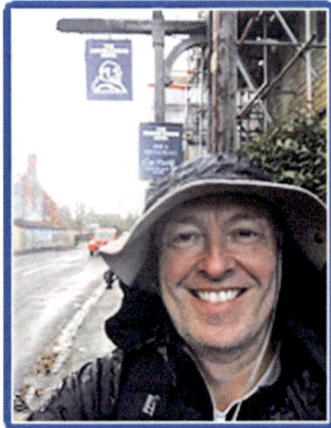

Arriving at the Shaven Crown.

With the 'Support Team'.

Hook Norton beer.

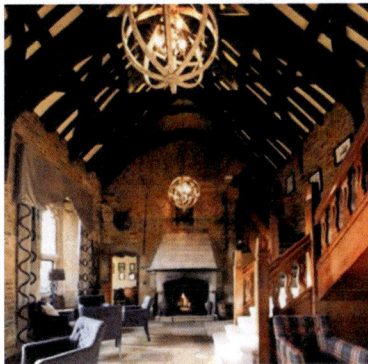

Picture from Shaven Crown website.

One Day Before Arriving at Milestone Five

Day 52. Wednesday 4 November, Shipton Under Wychwood to Oxford

I am now into the final two days of walking although I have two longish walks to conclude. The good thing is that with the 'support team' in attendance at least my rucksack will be transported. What a glorious sunny day with not a cloud in the sky when I set off. I have experienced all 'four seasons' of weather during my walk. Today it is freezing with a lovely frost on the ground, but my hands are red raw—they almost match my feet. I very nearly phone the 'support team' to bring my gloves but on one of those rare occasions common sense takes over … and I do not.

An observation from my walking in the Cotswolds is that I should ignore the mileage shown on signposts. At least twice over the last couple of days, I have been walking towards a village, I have seen a signpost indicating the number of miles until I reach the village, I walk further on until I reach the next signpost and the mileage outstanding has not changed. It's either incorrect calculations or I am in the middle of Groundhog Day. Tonight, is our final night away and tomorrow I am looking forward to sleeping in my own bed.

Thanks to the Hilton group for discounting the room rate at the Hampton Hilton in Oxford. I walk past my third and final football stadium—Oxford United. There are not many times that Oxford will be classed in the same bracket as Man Utd and Wolves. When we enter our room at the Hilton, we must remove the sticky tape that shows the room had been cleaned—it feels again like we were entering a disaster movie, and I guess to some extent we are in the middle of that now. I enjoy walking through Oxford city centre with the beautiful college buildings. Today I walk over 23 miles, so I am officially over the 600-mile target (601 to be exact) and the completion of the walk is tomorrow.

> Andrew: More familiar territory for me, having lived around Oxford for many years with lots of great and close friends. So, I picked up the phone more often again to know where he was, and I am sure my various descriptions of my own experience at various locations were well received by David. I do not recall lots of feedback on this matter from him, but I am sure they were. Obviously, lots of talk about the "finish tomorrow, however it does not really feel like a true finish from the conversation; there is no 'I'm delighted it's over' nor 'I am never doing this again' type discussion." It is all reflective of some highlights (which will have included my phone calls of course) and a slight uncomfortable ebb around back to normal, whatever normal means in these Corona-times...

News Headlines Context, 4 November 2020

In news headlines, Joe Biden delivers a 'victory speech' claiming Wisconsin and Michigan win. Joe Biden has hit out at Donald Trump's inflammatory and unfounded suggestions of voter fraud in the US election. The Democratic candidate did so during his latest speech, in which he confirmed that his campaign was feeling very confident about their chances of winning the presidency.

Mr Biden continued: "Here, the people rule. Power can't be taken or asserted. It flows from the people and it's their will that determines who will be the president of the United States and their will alone." Now, after a long night of counting, it's clear that we're winning enough states to reach 270 electoral votes needed to win the presidency. "I'm not here to declare that we've won, but I'm here to report that when the count is finished, we believe that we'll be the winners. EU chief admits 'big problem' amid 'danger' EU states could follow Brexit Britain's lead. Now, the new Vice-President of the European Economic and Social Committee (ESSC), Cillian Lohan, has warned a no-deal outcome would create 'enormous difficulties'. The Irish national also noted a 'problem' for the EU, which now 'affects all member states'. He said: 'Many British citizens voted in favour of Brexit because they no longer recognised themselves in the European institutions, they looked too disconnected from their reality'. It is a big problem, but it now affects all member states."

Mr Lohan went on to explain how the 'danger exists' for other member states to follow Britain and leave the EU.

Coronavirus Daily Context, 4 November 2020

Boris Johnson's new coronavirus measures have been approved by MPs by 516 votes to 38, but the Prime Minister has still been warned about a 'significant embarrassment' over the crunch decision in the House of Commons. On Saturday, the Prime Minister announced the UK would go into a second national lockdown amid growing concerns over rising coronavirus infections. But despite fears that some senior backbenchers could vote against the new measures, MPs approved the national lockdown. The new measures were passed by 516 votes to 38—a majority of 478. While it is not yet clear, which MPs voted against the second lockdown measures, it could have a significant impact if they are all Conservative politicians.

"Christmas banned: Council forbids traditional carol singing to halt coronavirus infections. Christmas celebrations have been banned in a seaside resort following fears they could trigger a spike in COVID-19 cases. Blackpool Council has banned its traditional carol singing and brass band performances following a debate this afternoon. The ban will stop a local Salvation Army Band playing on the four Saturdays before Christmas and on the 25th itself."

Tracking new cases 23,681; deaths 328

(Source: coronavirus.data.gov.uk)

So, the national lockdown will happen on the day I finish my walk, and there is unlikely to be any singing to celebrate my achievement. Perhaps I will sing to myself and that way it appears tuneful.

Frosty field.

Shipton.

Under Wychwood Leafield.

Leafield.

Leafield.

Leafield

University of Oxford Kassam Stadium.

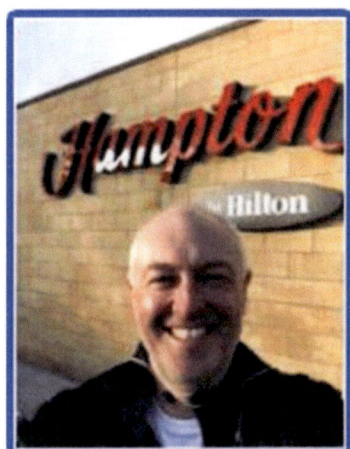

Arriving at Hampton by Hilton.

Day 53. Thursday 5 November, Oxford to Milestone 5

Hooray, the final day! Also, the start of national lockdown two. Wow, what a journey, and there have been a few times when I have not been sure I would get to this point. Another largely dry day, and I meet several people, which is a nice way to conclude. As I walk through the picturesque town of Dorchester, I am approached by a lady who went to school with Anne. She is out walking her dog and joins me on the walk as we go through the village, which is genuinely nice of her.

Then, as I walk through Shillingham, I spy Nigel and Julie who we had met in Marlow for lunch on my first practice walk. It is great to meet them, and they top up my water supply and give me a lovely home-cooked flapjack to keep me going on the final leg. The flapjack is cut into two equal squares, so my first thought is to briefly question whether I am depriving Nigel and Jonny of tonight's dessert; this is very quickly followed by my second thought, which is how yummy it is …. I also treat myself to a McDonald's breakfast bap and a latte en-route—all takeaway as a result of lockdown, but I manage to stand outside the restaurant and tap into the Wi-Fi.

So, I walk my 17 miles and beat my target! 618 miles in total.

Wooohooo!

Anne picks me up outside Reading, drops me 0.5 miles away from the **Royal Berkshire Hospital (Milestone five)** so that I can walk to the finishing line. It is easier to walk 0.5 miles than to park in Reading, so I arrive first. It is great that Sarah Critchley CEO of BIBS can join us (so we keep within COVID rules as only three of us are in the car park and socially distant). Sarah has been particularly proactive with her supportive comments and activity on social media.

I have a real mix of emotions—a sense of achievement (there were certainly times of doubt); elation, pain (in my feet), relief and joy that Anne and I have completed the challenge and will raise a decent sum for both charities which, along with the personal challenge was the main goal. Overall, I have been so lucky to have had the opportunity to undertake this challenge, and I have seen so many great sights and met so many fantastic people. Not today, and probably not for the next few days, but I will miss pounding the streets and the miles. I have walked 618 miles in 33 walking days although including my 2-week break and rest days it took 53 days from start to finish.

No question that this would be the fifth and final milestone—it goes back to one part of the root cause of my challenge, it's where the boys were born and the start of my fatherhood phase 23 years ago. It also very nearly completes a full circle or circuit walk (about 10 miles from home) from start to finish.

I want to say several "thank yous" as I could not have done this on my own. Thanks to Lisa who very kindly baked me a chocolate cake to celebrate the achievement, which is lovely—although when eating it, I half guiltily wish Matthew and James would still be at university or away with their friends, as it will disappear much more quickly with them at home. Thanks to everybody who followed the daily social media updates (no more breakfast photos to wade through); to everybody who has been generous to sponsor me, to all the pubs, cafes, B&Bs who have helped me during incredibly challenging times. I have already identified my next challenge—following the recent sad passing of Sir Sean Connery I am going to work my way through my James Bond DVD collection in film order.

Coronavirus Daily Context, 5 November 2020

"In news headlines London lockdown chaos: Police clash with protesters as tensions boil over in the capital. London has descended into chaos as police clash with people out on the streets protesting a second national lockdown. London police have been forced to intervene with large crowds on the capital's streets on Thursday night. Clashes broke out between the police and people protesting the second coronavirus lockdown. The footage is circulating on social media of police detaining individuals for their behaviour during the protests. Ministers… have listed specific occasions in which people can travel beyond their local area.

1. *Travelling to work where this cannot be done from home*
2. *Travelling for education and care*
3. *Visiting those in a support or childcare bubble*
4. *Hospital, GP and medical appointments*
5. *Buying goods or services from open premises, including essential retail*
6. *Spending time or exercise outdoors*
7. *Exercising or caring for a pet, or veterinary services"*

Tracking new cases 23,757; deaths 402
(Source: coronavirus.data.gov.uk)

Funnily enough, I am travelling back INTO my local area today—all within the context of the penultimate guideline for 'spending time or exercise outdoors'! It is just so weird. All my planning and the two-week gap I forced myself to take due to the impact on my feet, combined with the ongoing pandemic around me, which through the rapid infection rate and increase in deaths has resulted in national lockdown being imposed the very day that I achieve my goal.

It is simply weird! It feels like I am Laurel, and the pandemic is Hardy—the two things are symbiotic. When I started to plan my walk, I hardly thought about the pandemic. It was there in the background like a small boil. By the conclusion of my walk, the boil is more like the black death—a plague that cannot be ignored. It seeped into my walk at times, it threatened to catch up and overtake me—but I managed it and beat it, and I achieved what I set out to do.

Wow!

Nuneham Courtenay.

Meeting Nigel and Julie.

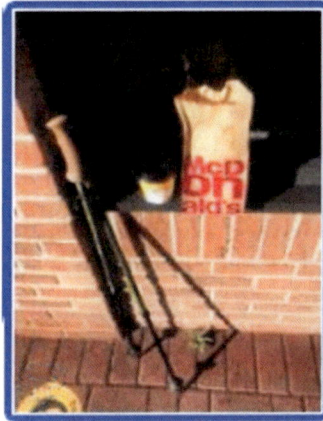

Giving in to temptation.

North Stoke.

Me walking in Shillingham

Royal Berkshire Hospital.

Arrived at destination.

Final leg!

Celebrating with Sarah Critchley and Anne.

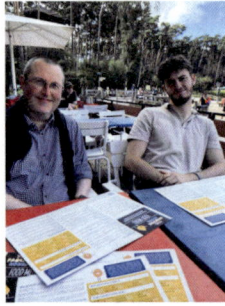

Tim: "I'm really proud of David's incredible effort to take on this challenge and raise money for charity. I'll admit I think his timing could have been much better, i.e. not during a pandemic, but his resolve was steadfast despite the many obstacles and especially sore feet. It's no surprise that he completed the trek on the same day the Government implemented the second national lock down!"

James: "It is a real testament to his character that he stuck through the recovery (very well supported by Mum who made sure he had everything he needed) and although he was still in pain, he completed the challenge like he said he would. Well done, Dad!"

Post Walk

Chocolate cake from Lisa

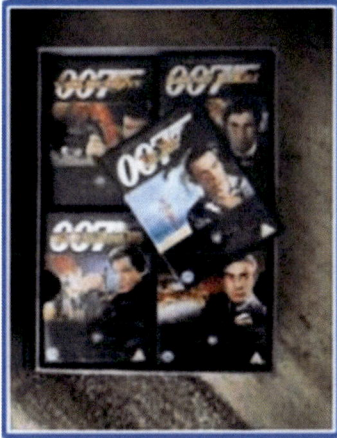

My next challenge

Conclusion

So now it is all over. My feet are recovering quickly, and it is nice to be home with family. It is hard to know where to start with my conclusions—I am delighted that I completed the walk as there were a couple of times when I had doubts; certainly, before I started, when I returned home at the end of week one and when I set off again after my 2 week recovery session. I am reminded again of the importance of having a plan (I had about 10 versions of the plan) but also being able to adapt the plan.

When I was re-planning the remainder of my walk during my 2 week break I listened to Anne (again) and reduced my daily mileage target from 20-30 to 15–20 miles and tried to schedule a rest day every 5 days. In the end, this helped me achieve the goal. Another big difference after week one was that I did not need to use taxis to transport my large rucksack—if I had done this all the way through then the costs would have been huge. A combination of the 'support team', using Paul and Alison as a base for a few days, help from mum and dad and carrying the larger load all helped me overcome that challenge.

I also had way too much stuff. I am still annoyed with myself that I ended up carrying several clothing items all around England and never actually wore them. Several people commented to me that they were surprised I did the walk on my own. I enjoyed it and never actually felt alone. Of course, I had the three phone calls a day with Andrew, daily with Anne, and intermittent calls with many others.

It was quite a personal journey and practically not many people could take five weeks (that turned into eight weeks) out of their lives with little preparation time. I had several people close to me say they wish they could have done what I was doing, and I had ongoing support from Anne and Andrew every day, my parents, and the boys frequently and met several friends and relatives on the way (but for COVID, it would have been many more).

COVID was an ever-present backdrop to my walk. It caused a lot of angst and as I have already mentioned, it restricted my ability to meet my family and friends—my cousin and my niece for example—but I was extremely fortunate to keep ahead of the local and national lockdowns. I recall visiting The Crown in Colne for example on the final night before they closed, and my last day walking was the day that the second national lockdown started. I did see and feel the impact of COVID directly on the tourism industry.

I think all the pubs and B&Bs were negatively impacted hugely—the lack of custom and lack of travellers had significantly reduced their income. Some were keen for the lockdown to come as it took the uncertainty away, others were expanding their takeaway business to supplement the losses. Regardless, so many helped and supported me while they themselves were in difficulty and that is utterly amazing and humbling.

Low moments? A few. Certainly, the day at the end of my first week around Grantham when I walked in flip flops and my Compeed plasters ended up sticking to the flip flops. And then walking 0.9 miles on the verge of the A1 dual carriageway with lorries speeding past me with only one or two metres gap—many flashing their headlights at me.

The same night when I made the decision to recuperate was also tough. I felt like a failure as I did not know whether my feet would take me on the whole journey. After all, I had only walked 134 miles of my 616 miles target, and I could hardly put my feet on the ground. Another low was when walking along the Manchester ship canal—yes in the rain, my route was blocked by a locked gate and the Google Maps on the phone would not give me an alternative route—that was highly annoying.

I had so many more highs than lows, however. The scenery stands out for one. There are so many beautiful sights and villages to explore, and the perspective is so different when walking as opposed to driving. I would never have noticed the beautifully trimmed hedges near Doncaster if I had been driving—my eyes would be on the road and sat nav. The impact that the sunshine can have in bringing the colours of the fields and trees to life I will never forget, and the creativity of many homes creating models or housing their robotic lawnmower in a kennel.

I loved reaching my destination each day as it was a mini-goal. I preferred to get up early and go (sacrificing a few breakfasts with this approach) but it meant that I could often arrive mid-afternoon and go through my stretch/relax routine.

I loved the hot, powerful shower at the end of each day and for sure when staying in the pubs I loved to have a couple of pints in the bar (with a roaring fire) to catch up on my emails and read my book before dinner.

I will treasure several of the nice cities, towns, villages that I visited—St Albans, Tewkesbury and Durham stand out, but also many of the smaller places that I had not visited before—Kineton, Prestbury to name but a few. The most enjoyable walking areas for me were the Yorkshire dales, the Cotswolds and a couple of days I did walking by the River Severn. Generally, the quieter areas with fantastic scenery although walking past Old Trafford was a real uplift as it was unexpected.

The overwhelming highlight must be the kindness and support I received from so many people. Many B&Bs, pubs and hotels donated during particularly challenging times; a number opened their premises just for me—often the owners were not even there. Many cafes donated coffee to me, and several waitresses donated their tips, which is incredibly generous. I was tempted to say 'notes only' when I saw copper coins going into my collection tin as I knew it was extra weight for me to carry—but seriously their contribution is hugely valued because tips are such a key component of their income.

The generosity of many strangers is also a highlight, I remember one lady handing me a £5 note from her car when she saw me hobbling along, another leaving a pub saw my collection tin and put in £6 without knowing why I was doing the walk or indeed for which charities. I had great support from Mick and Elaina with their advice and lending of kit; from Will who accompanied me on my training walks. I must call out thanks to Mum and Dad who called regularly and looked after me before the final leg, and to Matthew and James who joined me on the first day and then helped me with technology and route planning when needed.

Thanks to Tim for helping inspire me and to Andrew who phoned me two or three times every day and always brought a smile to my face (even the day I was lost in the rain by Manchester ship canal). Finally, to my support team—Anne—without whom I could not have completed the walk, who helped my packing, the sacrificed time she should have spent on her own businesses, joined me twice on different legs and was also on the phone every day.

So, I did it, 618 miles! We had an initial target of £2,000 but ended up raising over £5,000.

I have declared my next challenge already (working my way through the James Bond DVD collection) but I have an inkling of my next BIG challenge—please do not say anything to Anne …….

Mum and Dad: So proud he finished with all the odds against it and so proud of Anne who was such a fantastic support. He could not have done it without her!

List of Thank You's to B&B's, Pubs and Hotels

1. White Hart, Chalfont St Giles—D, B, B
2. White Hart, Welwyn—Bed
3. Orchard House, Royston—B&B
4. Sandford House, Huntingdon—Bed
5. Sibson Inn, Stibbington—Beer and tips
6. Dovecote Inn, Laxton—B&B
7. Barns Country Guesthouse, Morton—B&B
8. White Swan, Deighton—B&B
9. George Hotel, Easingwold—Discount
10. Victorian Town House, Durham—B&B
11. Redworth Hall, Newton Aycliffe—D, B, B
12. Eastfield Lodge, Leyburn—B&B
13. Fox & Hounds, Starbotton—Discount
14. The Crown, Colne—B&B
15. Eagle & Child, Ramsbottom—B&B
16. White House Manor, Prestbury—B&B
17. Borough Arms Hotel, Newcastle under Lyme—Discount
18. Britannia Hotel, Wolverhampton—B&B
19. Gainsborough House Hotel, Kidderminster—Bed
20. Tewkesbury Park, Tewkesbury—B&B
21. The Halfway House, Kineton—B&B
22. Shaven Crown, Shipton under Wychwood—B&B
23. Hilton Hampton, Oxford—Discount

A Tribute to the Unbelievable Kindness that I Experienced Across England During an Unbelievably Challenging Time!

Date	Location	Kindness Donated
13 September	White Hart, Chalfont St Giles	Bed, dinner, 2 pints
		Other guest donation
14 September	White Hart, Welwyn	Bed
15 September	Coffee shop, Buntingford	Waitress tips
15 September	Orchard House, Royston	Bed and breakfast
16 September	Coffee shop, Papworth Everard	Sandwich, coffee and
		Passer-by donation
	Sandford House, Huntingdon	Bed
17 September	Sibson Inn, Stibbington	Beer and tips
5 October	Dovecote Inn, Laxton	Bed and breakfast
6 October	Barns Country Guesthouse,	Bed and breakfast
7 October	Starbucks, Worksop	Latte
8 October	Florist/Coffee shop Askern	Latte and teacake
	White Swan, Deighton	Bed and breakfast
9 October	Fika café, Easingwold	Lunch and latte for me
	George Hotel, Easingwold	Discount
13 October	Pub, Durham	Waitress tips
	Victorian Town House	Bed and breakfast
15 October	Redworth Hall	Dinner, bed and
16 October	White Swan, Gilling West	Fishfinger sandwich and latte
		Passer-by donation

17 October	Eastfield Lodge, Leyburn	Bed and breakfast
18 October	Fox & Hounds, Starbotton	Discount
21 October	Furnishing/coffee shop, Colne	Soup, sandwich and
21 October	Crown, Colne	Bed and breakfast
22 October	Eagle & Child, Ramsbottom	Bed and breakfast
24 October	White House Manor, Prestbury	Bed and breakfast
25 October	Café, Prestbury	Latte and shortbread
26 October	Bull pub	Latte and soup and
	Borough Arms Hotel, Newcastle	Discount and donation
28 October	Costa, Shackerley	Latte
	Britannia, Wolverhampton	Bed and breakfast
29 October	Coffee shop, Kinver	Waitress tips
29 October	Gainsborough House,	Bed
1 November	Tewkesbury Park Hotel,	Bed and breakfast
2 November	Halfway House, Kineton	Bed and breakfast
3 November	Restaurant, Shipton under	Dinner for me and the
	Hooky speciality beers	Beer and glasses
	Shaven Crown, Shipton under	Bed and breakfast
4 November	Hilton Hampton, Oxford	Discount
5 November	Nigel and Julie	Flapjacks and water

Epilogue

Six months later some things have changed, and other things have not. As I write, we have recently come out of the third national lockdown and are within touching distance of being able to meet indoors socially and visit pubs again. We can visit the pub gardens and this weekend on 1 May 2021 will be my first visit to the Ship pub with Matthew and Anne (it turns out that James had a better offer!)

I am busy at work also. I applied on two occasions to the Royal Mail to become a postman and got rejected twice. Not even an interview. It could not have been due to a concern about my fitness having walked over 600 miles so it must have been based on a concern that I could successfully match the address on the envelope to the house sign…. I also got rejected by Tesco when I applied to pack the foodstuffs ready for home delivery. Once again not even an interview! In February, I set up my own business and now have several different business interests underway—all are interesting to me and provide both variety and challenge as I sought. I am helping three businesses to grow by using my contacts and marketing experience.

One is a small data science company that are looking to broaden their customer base. The second company helps small companies to refine their offering and facilitate meetings with board-level decision makers in FTSE 250 companies. The third company is focused on helping provide cyber security solutions to clients, and I am helping open doors for that. The fourth partnership is helping my financial advisor who has been great helping me with pension and investment opportunities to bring that service to others.

Finally—and this is the main area of my work focus—I have joined the Marketing Centre where I am a part-time director supporting SMEs with their marketing strategy and execution in order to grow their business. I won my first client in April and love meeting the team each week and building momentum. I have just won my second client. I enjoy the variety of meeting different teams and working in different businesses whilst having the flexibility to work with the afore-mentioned partners—and the odd round of golf with my father or the boys!

In the past twelve months, I have now achieved three of my life goals. One is the fundraising from the walk whilst achieving the 600 plus miles target. That is goal one. Goal two is now realised with this book. Who knows if anybody will buy it—well, I will be very disappointed if I don't sell seven copies to my parents (one copy each), my brothers, my lads and of course Anne! Full price too—no discount for family and friends. I had always wanted to write a book and try to get it published. I veered between a work of fiction (Jack Reacher type of novel), a book on leadership (I had the idea of writing to multiple leaders across sport and industry to note their wisdom and learning with the goal of finding common themes or lessons). I am happy with this, however, as my effort, and it ticks that box nicely and as a minimum it can be an interesting journal for future Fenton generations to read! The third goal—yes, I completed watching all the official James Bond movies over November/December 2020.

Feet update!

So, I am able to do everything I want and took up my daily five-mile run within about three weeks of completing the walk. I go running six days out of seven most weeks. I do have some twinges on my right foot and went to see a podiatrist recently. I have a small lump on the inside of my right foot caused by how the foot adapted to the stresses and strains I put on it. It does not hurt but I can feel it if I walk barefoot on a hard surface. The only cure is surgery, and I certainly do not want that—and do not need it at the moment.

I look back with fondness on my journey. I miss the moments traipsing the quiet country roads. I miss the great pubs and B&B's with the excitement of reaching a new destination every day (apart from the rest days). I miss being able to read my book with my evening meal and a pint. I do not miss the three daily calls from Andrew because even today I still get a regular facetime call. I am really glad I did it. And I am planning my next event—either a long bike ride as that will be less pressure on my feet or to run a half marathon—or maybe both!

Oh, and I have a 'boys' weekend booked for September—Matthew, James and Andrew all signed up. We are going… walking…